DATE DUE

The Pennypincher's Guide to Landscaping

The Pennypincher's Guide to Landscaping

Carol Boston

Prentice-Hall, Inc.

Englewood Cliffs, New Jersey

Prentice-Hall International, Inc., *London*
Prentice-Hall of Australia, Pty. Ltd., *Sydney*
Prentice-Hall Canada, Inc., *Toronto*
Prentice-Hall of India Private Ltd., *New Delhi*
Prentice-Hall of Japan, Inc., *Tokyo*
Prentice-Hall of Southeast Asia Pte. Ltd., *Singapore*
Whitehall Books, Ltd., *Wellington, New Zealand*
Editora Prentice-Hall do Brasil Ltda., *Rio de Janeiro*

©1985 *by*

Carol Boston
Englewood Cliffs, N.J.

Line art by Natalie Cecil

Library of Congress Cataloging in Publication Data

Boston, Carol.
  The pennypincher's guide to landscaping.

  Bibliography: p.
  Includes index.
  1. Landscape gardening. 2. Gardening. 3. Plants,
Ornamental. I. Title.
SB473.B59   1985   635.9   84-17775

ISBN 0-13-655937-9

ISBN 0-13-655929-8 {PBK}

Printed in the United States of America

DEDICATION

This book is dedicated to my parents, Frank and Irene Kajfosz, who instilled me with an extremely thrifty nature; to my husband, Nick, who "volunteered" to carry home countless half-dead plants; and to the late Marion Judin, who gave me confidence in myself and my writing ability.

ACKNOWLEDGMENT

Special thanks to Dona Allison and Wilbur Bluhm of the Marion County Extension Office, whose brains I picked unmercifully. Besides giving positive reinforcement, they were the source of much technical information. Without their assistance, even though my scrounging ability would not have been diminished, my ability to write about it coherently might have.

Foreword

This writing has been lying, only partly dormant, within Carol A. Boston for a number of years. Its impending eruption was signalled, much as our Mt. St. Helens signals its activity, by murmurings and other rather random but focused aggressiveness. The trigger that set off the outpouring of words and ideas may never be known. I suspect her restraints were finally overcome by her eagerness to share her knowledge, the belief that everyone should share the wonder of the plant world, and her amazement that anyone had less than an inviting yard.

Carol Boston is eminently qualified on her subject. She is an experienced and knowledgeable horticulturist. I would say her attraction to plants is a long-time love affair. She has traveled the backroads of Illinois during the winter with her house plants as companions. Her inquisitiveness and eagerness for new experiences have led her from those cold, snowy Illinois winters to the wet, mild, and lush Northwest.

While you, the reader, may rush through the book as through a novel, it behooves you to reread it at a slower pace. Dwell on the ideas and enthusiasm and you too will find greater value to her words.

As past president of the nonprofit South King County Arboretum Foundation, I appreciate the value of pinching pennies, smiling a lot, sweet talking, and trading plants.

As a lot, gardeners tend to be independent, and as one I doubted some of her methods. I do apologize, Ms. Boston. After trying them, I find they work.

Read and enjoy.

Curtiss E. Howard

Introduction: I Am What I Am

These days, with the price of everything skyrocketing, many people have found that they can't afford to do the landscape gardening they would like to do. I was one of those people. I looked at the magnificent pictures of well-landscaped homes and drooled. I wanted at least one of every lovely flower around. I drove down the streets, covetous of many of the yards I saw. But my husband and I had just bought our home, payments were high, and there was not much left over for landscape frills. So I sat in my dining room and looked out at the vast expanse of grass that was our yard. I dreamed of how I could transform it with just a few well-placed flowerbeds. I schemed about acquiring the plants to make those fantasies come true. That was two years ago. Today, my yard is an unusual combination of quiet shady places, sunny rock gardens, and fragrant borders.

A multitude of how-to books reveal secrets of growing various varieties of plants or of landscaping your yard, but most of these authorities assume that you have an abundance of money to spend on the exotic-sounding species they describe. This book neither stresses the growing requirements of individual plants nor gives a multitude of directions on how to draw landscape plans. What it does is give you a plan of action to follow if your garden fund is limited and if you are willing to exchange some time for cash on your landscape plant needs. Included in the chapters are hints on how you can acquire far more plant material than you ever thought you could afford. You will learn how to find reasonably priced plants and, quite often, even free plants. Naturally, all of the methods discussed will not fit your individual situation. Some people have more time, some are more outgoing, some are more particular about what types of plants they want in their yards. Just select the methods you feel most comfortable with and use them over and over.

THE LATIN CONNECTION

Throughout this book, you'll find both common names of plants and their botanical names—the Latin genus and species. You might think I use these "foreign" words to show off, but believe me, I don't. I'm including them so that if you're really interested in obtaining a specific plant, you indeed will end up with that particular plant and no other. For example, if I said the name "trout lily," would you know to which plant I was referring? Do you know that depending upon which part of the country you're in, the same plant is also called fawn lily, adder's tongue, dog-tooth violet, avalanche lily, or alpine lily? And it's not even related to violets. I call it dog-tooth violet because that's what I grew up calling it, but I also include the botanical name, *Erythronium*.

How about the flower, bachelor button? To my mother, it's a small, compact, yellow perennial plant. To me, it's an annual, often with blue flowers. What picture does it bring to your mind? To prevent confusion, if I talk about bachelor button, I'll also call it *Centaurea cyanus*—which is, by the way, the annual flower that can be blue, pink, rose, or white. But my mother calls that flower a ragged robin. And so it goes.

Common names are fine as long as all people concerned know of which plant they're speaking. But remember, what is called meadow saffron in Idaho may be known as autumn crocus in Kansas. To make certain you get exactly what you want, call it *Colchicum autumnale*. Then anyone can look up the name in a reference book if he or she is not familiar with it and give you what you're really looking for. And don't be shy about pronouncing the words—almost everyone mispronounces some of them unless he or she's a Latin scholar or the like. It's better to mispronounce the Latin than to get the wrong plant.

Have I convinced you of the importance of botanical names? I rest my case.

Now that you know why I use these names, let me explain a little about their personalities. Hopefully, this will help make those funny-looking words a little more palatable.

The botanical terms I'll use generally are in two parts. The first, which is always capitalized, is the plant's genus. A genus is a group of plants having one or more common characteristics. It can be compared to a person's last name. Mine is "Boston." Many others in my family have the same last name, but I'm the only one named "Carol." The species of the plant is the second term and can be compared to my first name, "Carol." It, however, is never capitalized.

Sometimes a third word is used. It is called a variety and would equate to my middle name, 'Ann.' If I had a cousin with the name, "Carol Boston," my middle name, 'Ann,' would distinguish between the two of us. Varietal names are put in single quotations.

Are you at a complete loss? Written in correct botanical form, my name would be *Boston* (genus) *carol* (species) 'Ann' (variety). Or, substituting a plant, an ever red Japanese maple would be, *Acer* (genus) *palmatum* (species) 'ever red' (variety). This is just the taxonomist's way of pinning down a specific plant.

Sometimes you can tell a whole lot about a plant from its botanical name. Often the words mean something specific about that plant. They can indicate where the plant originally came from, what it looks like, or what kind of conditions it needs to do well. For example, the species *rubens* means that some part of the plant—perhaps the leaves or flowers—is red. If you have no place in your landscape for a red-hued plant, your best bet is to keep away from any plant that has *rubens* in its name.

Montanus tells you that the plant came from the mountains, *canadensis* from Canada, and *chinensis* from China. This gives you a clue as to the type of conditions a plant needs to thrive. Chances are, for example, if you see a plant with *canadensis* in its name, it won't do well in the desert regions of the country.

You'll find that the suffix *oides* is used often. This means "like" or "resembling." So if you saw the name *jasminoides*, you'd know that in some way this plant is like a jasmine—perhaps in growth habit or in fragrance.

Contortus indicates that the plant shape is contorted. This is nice to know, especially since sometimes small plants do not show their contortion until they're larger than the size you would generally purchase. If you saw a small plant at a nursery and did not know its name, you might think that it would grow up to be straight and tall. However, the minute you see the word *contortus*, you'd know better.

Now here's a test question to see if you've been paying attention. If you were looking for a plant with very fine, feathery foliage, would you be more likely to pick the one with the word *plumosus* or *barbatus* in its name? *Plumosus* means plumed; *barbatus*, barbed. If you answered correctly, go on to the next page. If not, reread this section on botanical names and give yourself two slaps with an *Opuntia bigelovii* pad.

Of course, some botanical names tell you nothing about the plant, but it's still a good idea to pay attention just in case they do. Consider coralbells, a perennial plant. Its botanical name is *Heuchera sanguinea*. To me, those words don't mean a thing. Perhaps to you Latin buffs they do, but there aren't any bells ringing in my head.

Of course, even the botanical names aren't foolproof. Larkspur, for example, was formerly named *Delphinium ajacis*. Now it's *Consolida ambigua*. Perhaps *ambigua* is included in its name to mean "not certain or unclear." I don't know. I'm sure the taxonomists who changed the name had very good reasons. Perhaps it was changed because the plant isn't related to delphiniums after all. This might bring about a mix-up, however, if you were reading an older book and the former name was used. But there are really not very many cases like this, and botanical names are a lot less of a mess than common ones. Some books will even list the former name to help keep you straight. All my botanical names have been taken from *Hortus Third: A Concise Dictionary of Plants Cultivated in the U.S. and Canada* by Liberty Hyde Bailey (New York: MacMillan Publishing Company, 1976.) This book is the recognized authority in the field.

To prevent confusion, I'd like to explain a term I'll be using throughout this book before you have a chance to wonder about it. When I mention the genus of a plant often I'll use the term *various* rather than list a number of species after it. This just means that many of the species fall into whatever category I'm discussing at the time. For example, I mention lavender as a good plant in rocky environments. Rather than list *Lavandula angustifolia, Lavandula dentata, Lavandula latifolia,* and *Lavandula stoechas*, which are all good plants for rocky soil, I just say *Lavandula* various. If, however, only one of these lavenders were appropriate for a rocky area, I would only mention, for instance, *Lavandula dentata*.

Got it? If you really understand all this botanical name stuff, congratulations. It took me quite a while to assimilate it all. Don't worry if you don't, though. You'll catch on as you go along. It's not really imperative that you understand; it just makes it easier to get what you want (see Table I-1).

TABLE I-1

Definitions of Some Botanical Terms

albus: white

americana: of America

angustifolius: narrow leaves

arborescens: treelike

autumnale: autumn blooming

candidus: pure white, shiny

compactus: compact, dense

concolor: one color

cordatus: heart-shaped

dendron: tree

discolor: two separate colors

edulus: edible

elegans: elegant

floridus: flowering tree

glaucous: as though sprinkled with light powder

grandiflora: large-flowered

humilis: low, small, humble

insularis: of islands

littoralis: of seashores

mollis: soft or soft and hairy

multiflora: many flowers

nanus: dwarf

nutans: nodding, swaying

officinalis: medicinal

parvifolius: small-leafed

patens: open, spreading

procumbens: trailing

Contents

1

Extra, Extra, Read All About It!

In the Introduction, I promised that this book would pertain primarily to acquiring landscape material at very low cost. Before you actually start the acquisition, however, it's important that you know exactly what you want and then zero in on those plants and only those plants. This is a lesson I didn't learn until I had a patio full of plants I didn't really want. I didn't even know where to put them.

HOLD YOUR HORSES

Before you get anything, decide what results you want. Do you want a yard that is manicured and sculptured, one that takes a good deal of time to maintain and has everyone "oohing" and "aahing"? Or do you want a functional yard, a place where children could play and explore, that takes a minimum of maintenance? Perhaps you want a garden with an abundance of flowers for cutting and for dried arrangements through which you could wander, enjoying and absorbing all the delicious fragrances. If you don't know for sure, decide, and before you purchase a single plant, check the local library. There you will find scores of books that will help you get started in the right direction. There are books about shade gardens, sun gardens, easy maintenance gardens, formal gardens, rose gardens—in fact, about almost any type of garden you can name.

I spent just five minutes examining our local library's titles and here's what I found:

Gardening for Fragrance Indoors and Out
Nelson Coon
Doubleday & Company, Inc. 1975

Gardening in Small Spaces
Jack Kramer
HP Books 1979

Gardening in the Shade
Harriet K. Morse
Charles Scribner's Sons 1962

Gardening with Perennials Month by Month
Joseph Hudak
New York Times Book Co. 1976

Ideas for Hanging Gardens
Ideas for Desert Gardening
Ideas for Japanese Gardens
Editors of *Sunset Books & Sunset Magazine*
Lane Publishing Co. 1975, 1967, and 1972 respectively

Low Maintenance Gardening
Editors of *Sunset Books & Sunset Magazine*
Lane Books 1974

Rock Gardening: A Guide to Growing Alpines and Other
Wildflowers in the American Garden
H. Lincoln Foster
Houghton Mifflin Company 1968

Shady Gardens, How to Plan and Grow Them
Emily Seaber Parcher
Brandon Press, Inc. 1972

Successful Gardening in the Shade
Helen Van Pelt Wilson
Doubleday & Company, Inc. 1975

Successful Gardening with Limited Water
Margarot Tipton Wheatly
Woodbridge Press Publishing Company 1978

Shade Gardens
Rock & Water Gardens
Etc.
Time-Life Series
Time-Life Books 1979

Your library probably has a similar collection of such books. Do some reading and make good use of them.

You need to consider many aspects when you decide which type of landscape will fit your life style. Do you have young children or pets? If so, you'll need to find sturdy plants and incorporate into your plan at least one "little people's" play area. Consider a sandbox or even just a few well-placed tree stumps for your children to play on. Hundreds of alternatives exist to the standard metal gym set. Many of them are even preferred by children.

If you do a lot of outdoor entertaining, you'll need a patio or deck large enough to hold outdoor furniture, a barbeque grill, potted plants, plus an assortment of guests. To me, parties are less fun when I'm crammed shoulder to shoulder with a large potted fuschia. Think also about such things as how convenient it is to get from the kitchen to the patio.

How about taking into account the needs of teenagers: Do they play croquet, badminton, or basketball? Do they have friends over for outdoor parties? Why not ask them what ideas they have. Perhaps you could get them involved in planning their own special area.

Are you interested in having a large vegetable garden? Is there an area on your property where such a garden could be screened off from the rest of the landscaping? Some gardeners are so proud of their vegetable gardens that they don't mind having them as a focal point of their yard. Mine is not exactly a thing of beauty in the summer because weeding it always seems to come in as a low priority. After the first frost, it also looks a tad pathetic, so I try to keep mine out of sight as much as possible.

Consider the architecture of your house. What kind of landscaping would fit with it? If you are leaning toward a formal Italian look and your house has rough-sawn cedar siding, I'd suggest either a move or a change in landscaping plans.

Many readers will not be starting with a yard devoid of any landscape plants, so they need to think about this. Decide which are worth keeping, but don't be too hasty about cutting down any large trees or shrubs. It will take either years to get any that size again, or a lot of money to have them moved in. Wouldn't it be better to do some pruning first to determine if a little shaping will help the plant become more acceptable?

What kind of liabilities do you have in your yard? Is there a large overhang from the house roof? If so, and you plant under it, you'll have a lot of hand watering to do, even in the wet season. Do your neighbors have an unattractive shed that you can see from your deck? Plan to plant a fast-growing screen or to erect a barrier to block it out. Do you have an area that stands with water whenever it rains? Would you rather plant a bog garden or improve the drainage? Is a steep slope causing erosion problems? You can change the slope or perhaps plant a ground cover to control the erosion.

How much effort are you willing to expend on landscaping and maintenance chores? Think not only of time, but of energy and money as well. Ask yourself if you really enjoy pruning, trimming, and spraying or if you would rather spend that time doing something else.

THE BIG STEP

Now it's time to get to work. Measure your property and make yourself a map that includes all existing buildings and large plants. Then delineate three basic areas—the public area, usually found in the front of the house radiating around the entryway; the living area, consisting of patio or deck and grounds around it; and the service area, consisting of garden, storage, and work areas. Circle each area on the map with a different color pencil.

Once this is completed, pencil in the existing walkways that connect these areas, or put in walkways you would like to have. Remember that straight lines are fine for formal landscapes but that gently curving ones fit better with more naturalistic styles.

If you have special problem areas such as a rocky or very wet section or a particularly bad view to block out, mark them on your map too. Once you have the map well in hand, put in some of your own ideas for bed placement, play areas, etc. Then go out into your yard and with a flexible hose mark off some of the ideas you drew. They'll look a lot different in real life than on the map. Change the lines you drew with the hose until you're satisfied with the result; then put your changes on the map.

Once you have delineated areas and beds, you can begin to think about what sort of plant material you should incorporate. Please remember that you don't have to put all the plants in at once. This can and should be a progressive plan in order to give yourself time to adjust to the changes and see them as they really are. Start with the larger items and work down to the smallest, filling in as you go. This will give you more opportunity to change your mind. And, if you're like I am, that will be often.

If you really want to do a bang-up job and are serious about your landscaping project, I would highly recommend that you purchase a publication that is aimed toward helping you with your basic plan. I don't often advocate purchasing a book because I feel there are more than enough available from the local library that are not only free but extremely adequate for any project I undertake. But in this case, I definitely would suggest the purchase of a publication entitled *Homescaping*. It has been published in cooperation with the United States Department of Agriculture and several state extension offices. The cost is only $2.25, which includes postage. Write to Mary Winger, the extremely nice, helpful lady in the Bulletin Room at Box 3313,

University Station, Laramie, Wyoming 82071. Make your check payable to the Agriculture Revolving Fund #54–3219. And yes, you can tell her I sent you.

Not only does this booklet take you by the hand through the perils of constructing your plot plan, but it also includes a triangle, straight-edge, and French curve to make certain you get the job done right. It comes complete with tracing paper, graph paper, and instructions that even I can understand. One of the most helpful things included is a template of symbols or shapes for drawing different types and sizes of plants. Use these to make cut-outs that you can move around your plan until you get the effect you want. Sure beats penciling them in and erasing until you're satisfied.

So with this booklet, all you need to start on your landscaping plan is a pencil and tape measure for measuring your property.

THE UNDECIDED

For those of you who are still undecided about exactly which effect you would like to achieve, here are some ideas for you to think about.

A rustic garden can use a curving dry stream bed of rocks as a focal point. Rough-hewn benches and fences will set it off, with boulders used as accents. You can make walkways of tree rounds and raised beds with railroad ties. A bird feeding area might be a highlight. Naturalize some spring bulbs for early color, and add sour gum (*Nyssa sylvatica*) for coppery red fall color and male maidenhair tree (*Ginkgo biloba*) for yellow autumn foliage. Cotoneaster (*Cotoneaster* various) and firethorn (*Pyracantha* various) will provide colorful berries, and large trees such as oak (*Quercus* various) and pine (*Pinus* various) can form the structure. This will be a relatively maintenance-free start to a rustic garden and would suit itself particularly well to a dry, rocky environment, although it would be appropriate in other areas as well (see Figures 1-1 and 1-2).

If an oriental effect is more to your liking, consider as a focal point a small teahouse with a bamboo fence in the background. Water basins and stone lanterns can act as accents, with an emphasis on stone beds, pebbles, sand, and boulders. Oriental landscapes are predominantly green with a few pastel blossoming

Figures 1-1, 1-2. Rustic settings (*Oregon State Fair*).

plants. Think about graceful clumps of bamboo (*Bambusa* various), dwarf junipers (*Juniperus* various), and feathery, pyramidal plume Japanese cedar (*Cryptomeria japonica* 'Elegans'). If you want fall color, plant a Japanese maple (*Acer palmatum*). Use flowering almond (*Prunus triloba*), Japanese flowering cherry (*Prunus serrulata*), or flowering quince (*Chaenomeles* various) for pastel blooms. Here is the beginning of another fairly low-maintenance garden (see Figures 1-3 and 1-4).

You don't have to have a lot of money or live in the tropics to obtain a tropical effect. Construct a lanai with a small footbridge over a trickle of water, or maybe even a tiny waterfall, and you have the base. Add some colorful tuberous cannas (*Canna* various) whose leaves resemble those of a banana, or caster bean (*Ricinus communis*), an annual that will produce huge tropical-looking leaves and grow six to fifteen feet in one season. Top it off with a healthy sprinkling of some of the many available types of ferns. For large plants, consider catalpa (*Catalpa* various) with its large heart-shaped leaves and trumpet-shaped flowers, or loquat (*Eriobotrya japonica*) with small fragrant flowers among big, leathery leaves. To bring in a touch of the truly exotic, add some groupings of iris (*Iris* various), whose flowers, at first glance, resemble orchids. This should get you off to a good and inexpensive tropical start (see Figures 1-5, 1-6, and 1-7).

If you're not a gardener and never want to be, here are some ideas for a low-maintenance landscape. Keep lawns, flower beds, and hedges completely out of the picture. Concentrate on plenty of ground covers whether they be pebbles and barkdust or plants such as sedum (*Sedum* various), cotoneaster (*Cotoneaster* various), or lilyturf (*Liriope* various). Add some easy-care trees, shrubs, and vines such as Russian olive (*Elaeagnus angustifolia*), vine maple (*Acer circinatum*), cinquefoil (*Potentilla* various), Japanese barberry (*Berberis thunbergii*), and trumpet creeper (*Campsis* various), and voilá, you're on your way to the beach (or wherever else you go when you don't have yard work to do).

For an elegant, formal look, keep balance, symmetry, and repetition in mind. One side of your landscape should mirror the other. Color needs to be kept in larger masses, as in a formal rose garden with the bushes in neat rows. Consider an herb garden here along with a piece of central statuary or fountain for focus. Symmetrical brick paths edged by sheared boxwood hedges will

Figures 1-3, 1-4. Oriental gardens (*Oregon State Fair*).

Figures 1-5, 1-6, 1-7. Tropical effects (*Oregon State Fair*).

Figure 1-8. A formal rose garden (*Oregon State Fair*).

also fit well. Sundials and cast- or wrought-iron benches could add interest points. Boxwood (*Buxus* various), privet (*Ligustrum* various), Surinam cherry (*Eugenia uniflora*), or Pacific wax myrtle (*Myrica californica*) can all be clipped to form topiary shapes. Because of the constant clipping and pruning to keep the proper shapes, this is a fairly high-maintenance landscape and tends to be more expensive than the others (see Figures 1-8, 1-9, and 1-10).

One of my favorite types of landscaping is an English cottage garden. This should bring to mind visions of thatched roofs and rambling brick paths—an old-fashioned, pastoral setting. Several kinds of gardens can be included within this one. Perhaps a small area can be devoted to cut flowers. Consider cosmos (*Cosmos bipinnatus*), butterfly weed (*Asclepias tuberosa*), and tricolor chrysanthemum (*Chrysanthemum carinatum*). Plan a fragrant garden in another section. Plant heliotrope (*Heliotropium arborescens*), Korean spice viburnum (*Viburnum carlesii*), and mignonette (*Reseda odorata*). Plants cultivated for their drying potential can inhabit another part of the landscaping. Try love-in-a-mist (*Nigella damascena*), bells of Ireland (*Moluccella laevis*), and French hydrangea (*Hydrangea macrophylla*) here. An herb garden can be planted close to the kitchen for convenience. Such plants as basil (*Ocimim basilicum*), French tarragon (*Artemisia*

Figures 1-9, 1-10. Small formal gardens (*Oregon State Fair*).

Figure 1-11. A colorful perennial garden with an annual flower border (*Jane Kailing*).

dracunculus), and lovage (*Levisticum officinale*) will become indispensable to the cook. And, of course, no English cottage garden can be complete without a selection of perennial flowers. The list is endless, but a few of my favorites include flax (*Linum perenne*), Japanese anenome (*Anenome hybrida*), and bellflower (*Campanula* various). The English cottage garden entails a fair amount of maintenance, but it's worth it for all the pleasure it brings (see Figure 1-11 and Tables 1-1, 1-2, 1-3, 1-4, and 1-5).

If you aren't enamored with any of my ideas, or if you want more, look in your local library for an excellent book called *100 Garden Plans* by Andrew R. Addkison (New York: Random House, 1977.) This book, unlike many others whose plans are so elaborate that they're intimidating to the novice, contains simple, small-scale plans that also include plant names. Everything from a beginner's garden and children's secret garden to a courtyard garden and semiformal garden is discussed. In addition, there are ninety-six other ideas in easy-to-understand form. To me, using this book is like putting together a simple jigsaw puzzle. It's fun and entertaining. Pick out the pieces that you like from the book and fit them into your landscape plan. You can choose one plan for the front entrance, another for the deck area, a third for the children's spot. It's all mix and match.

TABLE 1-1

A Cutting Garden

NAME	TYPE	COMMENTS
Balloon flower (*Platycodon grandiflorus*)	Perennial	Long bloom period
Bridal-wreath (*Spiraea* various)	Deciduous shrub	Branches graceful in arrangements
Butterfly weed (*Asclepias tuberosa*)	Perennial	Flowers and seedpods used
China aster (*Callistephus chinensis*)	Annual	Look for wilt-resistant varieties
Cosmos (*Cosmos bipinnatus*)	Annual	Self-seeds
Cotoneaster (*Cotoneaster* various)	Shrub and ground cover	Branches useful for late season berries
Delphinium (*Delphinium* various)	Perennial	Taller varieties need staking
Flowering almond (*Prunus triloba*)	Deciduous tree	Early spring flowers
Geum (*Geum quellyon*)	Perennial	Long bloom period
Grape myrtle (*Lagerstroemia indica*)	Shrub	Needs heat to bloom well
Magnolia (*Magnolia* various)	Tree or shrub	Foliage also useful
Mealy-cup sage (*Salvia farinacea*)	Perennial	Violet-blue spikes
Mexican sunflower (*Tithonia rotundifolia*)	Perennial	Drought- and heat-tolerant
Oleander (*Nerium oleander*)	Evergreen shrub	Drought- and heat-tolerant
Pot marigold (*Calendula officinalis*)	Annual	Self-seeds
Snapdragon (*Antirrhinum majus*)	Perennial	Look for rust-resistant varieties
Tricolor chrysanthemum (*Chrysanthemum carinatum*)	Annual	Long-lasting cut flowers

TABLE 1-2

A Fragrant Garden

NAME	TYPE	COMMENTS
Flowering tobacco (*Nicotiana* various)	Annual	Some varieties more fragrant than others
Heliotrope (*Heliotropium arborescens*)	Perennial	Does not make a good cut flower
Honeysuckle (*Lonicera* various)	Shrub or vine	Attracts humming birds
Korean spice viburnum (*Viburnum carlesii*)	Deciduous shrub	Very sweet fragrance in spring
Lantana (*Lantana montevidensis*)	Annual	Very strong fragrance
Lily-of-the-valley (*Convallaria majalis*)	Bulb	Ground cover with spring flowers
Mexican orange (*Choisya ternata*)	Evergreen shrub	Long bloom period
Mignonette (*Reseda odorata*)	Annual	Flowers not impressive but fragrance is
Mock orange (*Philadelphus* various)	Deciduous shrub	Really smells like orange flowers
Pink (*Dianthus* various)	Annual or perennial	Clove-scented
Stock (*Matthiola incana*)	Annual	Spicy-sweet fragrance; good cut flower
Summer lilac (*Buddleia davidii*)	Deciduous shrub	Clusters of midsummer flowers
Summer phlox (*Phlox paniculata*)	Perennial	Self seeds but does not come true from them
Sweet box (*Sarcococca hookerana*)	Evergreen shrub	Ground cover with spring flowers
Sweet rocket (*Hesperis matronalis*)	Perennial	Old time plant
Wallflower (*Cheiranthus cheiri*)	Perennial	Sweet fragrance in many colors
Winter daphne (*Daphne odora*)	Evergreen shrub	Pale pink flowers in early spring

TABLE 1-3

A Dried Flower Garden

NAME	TYPE	COMMENTS
Baby's-breath (Gypsophila paniculata)	Perennial	Cut before fully open
Bells-of-Ireland (Moluccella laevis)	Annual	Apple green flowers
Common immortelle (Xeranthemum annuum)	Annual	Flowers are pale, papery bracts
Crested cockscomb (Celosia cristata)	Annual	Velvety, fan-shaped flower
Everlasting (Helipterum roseum)	Annual	Cut when fully opened
Hydrangea (Hydrangea macrophylla)	Deciduous shrub	Color may depend on soil acidity
Globe amaranth (Gomphrena globosa)	Annual	Papery, cloverlike heads
Globe thistle (Echinops exaltatus)	Perennial	Holds blue color when dried
Job's-tears (Coix lacryma-jobi)	Perennial grass	Cut seedpods before dry
Love-in-a-mist (Nigella damascena)	Annual	Use seedpods
Love-lies-bleeding (Amaranthus caudatus)	Annual	Drooping, tassel-like flowers
Money plant (Lunaria annua)	Biennial	Self seeds
Plumed cockscomb (Celosia plumosa)	Annual	Plume-like, feathery flowers
Red-osier dogwood (Cornus sericea)	Deciduous shrub	Red twigs hold color when dry
Sea lavendar statice (Limonium sinuatum)	Annual	Makes good fresh cut flower
Strawflower (Helichrysum bracteatum)	Annual	Pick flowers before fully open
Yarrow (Achillea millefolium)	Perennial	Several colors available

TABLE 1-4

An Herb Garden

NAME	TYPE	COMMENTS
Basil (Ocimum basilicum)	Annual	Makes a nice border
Bee balm (Monarda didyma)	Perennial	Minty flavor but not as invasive as mints
Borage (Borago officinalis)	Annual	Cucumber flavor
Caraway (Carum carvi)	Biennial	Self-seeds
Chervil (Anthriscus cerefolium)	Annual	Finely cut leaves; good edging plant
Chive (Allium schoenoprasum)	Perennial	Oniony flavor, forms clumps
Dill (Anethum graveolens)	Annual	Self-seeds
French tarragon (Artemisia dracunculus)	Perennial	Has a sprawly habit
Lemon balm (Melissa officinalis)	Perennial	Lemon flavor, related to mint
Lovage (Levisticum officinale)	Perennial	Celery flavor
Origanum (Origano vulgare)	Perennial	Very drought-tolerant
Parsley (Petroselinum crispum)	Biennial	Many varieties available
Rosemary (Rosmarinus officinalis)	Evergreen shrub	Drought-tolerant; attracts bees
Sage (Salvia officinalis)	Perennial	Very drought-tolerant
Salad burnet (Poterium sanguisorba)	Perennial	Lacy leaves; cucumber flavor
Thyme (Thymus various)	Evergreen perennial	Hundreds of kinds to choose from
Winter savory (Satureia montana)	Perennial	Good as border

TABLE 1-5

A Perennial Garden

NAME	BLOOM TIME	COMMENTS
Aster (Aster various)	Fall	Over 500 varieties available
Astilbe (Astilbe various)	Late spring	Graceful, plume-like flowers
Bellflower (Campanula various)	Early summer	Varied sizes and shapes
Blanket flower (Gaillardia grandiflora)	All season	Flowers first year from seed
Christmas rose (Helleborus niger)	Winter	Evergreen
Chrysanthemum (Chrysanthemum morrifolium)	Fall	A large variety of colors
Columbine (Aquilegia various)	Late Spring	Self-seeds
Dead nettle (Lamium maculatum)	Grown for foliage	Silvery markings on leaves
Dwarf plumbago (Ceratostigma plumbaginoides)	Late summer	Ground cover with intense blue flowers
Flax (Linum perenne)	Summer	Airy habit; long blooming period
Japanese anenome (Anenome hybrida)	Fall	Good for shade
Lavender cotton (Santolina chamaecyparissus)	Grown for foliage	Makes good edging or hedge
Moss pink (Phlox subulata)	Spring	Good for edging
Plantain lily (Hosta various)	Grown for foliage	Very trouble-free
Rue (Ruta graveolens)	Grown for foliage	Graceful foliage
Shasta daisy (Chrysanthemum superbum)	Summer	Many different varieties available
Wormwood (Artemisia various)	Grown for foliage	Silvery leaves; drought-resistant

A "DIRTY" WORD

What if you have specific problems with your soil? This is something you should be alert to before you start to gather your plants. Ask gardening friends, nursery owners, or the county agent if you're not certain about specific local soil problems.

For example, if you live in a light rainfall area, you might have an alkalinity problem with your soil. Plants such as camellia (*Camellia* various) and rhododendron (*Rhododendron* various) won't grow well, so don't even try. Some gardeners recommend trying to amend this type of soil with sulfur or peat, but that gets too expensive for my budget. One of the least expensive solutions is to raise your beds and improve the soil in them by adding compost and other organic materials such as leaves, straw, manure, and so on. However, it will not be a project that can be completed overnight. It might take years to totally correct the average size lot, but don't despair, there are plenty of plants that will not only tolerate, but actually thrive in alkaline soil (see Table 1-6). And since your soil is probably only slightly alkaline, you should have even less of a problem. If you want to be certain about it, however, purchase a soil test kit at a nursery and check it out.

Salinity, an excess of salts, can be a problem in some arid areas. If you have adequate drainage, you can leach the salts out of your soil periodically by heavy watering. Of course, as you take out the salts, you're also taking out the nutrients, so it's important to return them to the soil. Adding organic matter is once again an answer. Another solution would be to concentrate on gardening in containers.

In very dry areas, it is important to add organic matter to the soil because it will help to retain moisture, which is good for both the plants and your pocketbook if you have to pay for water. Mulching will also help to hold moisture in and reduce the loss of soil moisture from evaporation. Grass lawns are notorious for the large amounts of water they require, so it might be wise to reduce the amount of grass in the landscape and replace it with ground covers, low shrubs, brick, or stones (see Table 1-7). These will allow the rain to enter the soil but will slow it down and prevent run-off and consequent soil erosion. Even extremely dry areas have a rainy season, so take advantage of this time of year and plant just before you know the rains will begin. This will get your plants off to a good start and you'll save money by not having to

TABLE 1-6

Alkaline-Tolerant Plants

NAME	TYPE	COMMENTS
African daisy (*Arctotis* hybrids)	Annual	Self-seeds
Bottlebrush (*Callistemon* various)	Evergreen shrub	Watch for iron deficiency
California juniper (*Juniperus californica*)	Evergreen tree	Very tough tree
Coyote bush (*Baccharis pilularis*)	Evergreen shrub	Look for male plants
Cupflower (*Nierembergia hippomanica* 'violacea')	Perennial	Long bloom period
Desert gum (*Eucalyptus rudis*)	Evergreen tree	Very tough tree
Flame vine (*Pyrostegia venusta*)	Evergreen vine	Blooms in fall
Honey locust (*Gleditsia triacanthos*)	Deciduous tree	Has thorns
Jerusalem cherry (*Solanum pseudocapsicum*)	Evergreen; perennial	Fruit poisonous; self-seeds
Marguerite (*Chrysanthemum frutescens*)	Perennial	Very fast-growing
Mexican creeper (*Antigonon leptopus*)	Deciduous vine	Very fast grower
Natal plum (*Carissa grandiflora*)	Evergreen	Fragrant flowers; edible fruit
Olive (*Olea europaea*)	Evergreen tree	Fruitless varieties available
Osage orange (*Maclura pomifera*)	Deciduous tree	Has thorns
Pomegranate (*Punica granatum*)	Deciduous tree	Showy flowers
Pot marigold (*Calendula officinalis*)	Annual	Self-seeds
Wisteria (*Wisteria* various)	Deciduous	Watch for iron deficiency

TABLE 1-7

Plants for Ground Cover

NAME	TYPE	COMMENTS
Carpet bugleweed (Ajuga reptans)	Evergreen	Can be mowed
Christmas fern (Polystichum acrostichoides)	Semi-evergreen	Needs shade and moisture
Common wood fern (Dryopteris spinulosa)	Semi-evergreen	Needs shade and moisture
Creeping cotoneaster (Cotoneaster adpressus)	Evergreen	Red berries
Creeping St.-John's-wort (Hypericum calycinum)	Evergreen	Good for erosion control
Creeping thyme (Thymus praecox arcticus)	Evergreen	Takes light foot traffic
Dichondra (Dichondra micrantha)	Evergreen	Lawn substitute in warm winter areas
Dwarf broom (Genista pilosa)	Deciduous	Yellow late-spring flowers
European cranberry (Viburnum opulus 'Nanum')	Deciduous	Has no flowers or fruit
Japanese knotweed (Polygonum cuspidatum 'compactum')	Deciduous	Good for erosion control
Juniper (Juniperus various)	Evergreen	Drought-resistant
Peppermint (Mentha piperita)	Perennial	Very fast grower
Speedwell (Veronica incana)	Evergreen	Can be mowed
Spring cinquefoil (Potentilla tabernaemontani)	Evergreen	Fast grower; yellow flowers
Stonecrop (Sedum various)	Succulent	Drought-tolerant
Thrift (Armeria maritima)	Evergreen	Makes tidy mounds
Wintercreeper (Euonymus fortunei 'radicans')	Evergreen	Sprawling vine

TABLE 1-8

Plants for Dry Areas

NAME	TYPE	COMMENTS
Amur maple (*Acer ginnala*)	Deciduous tree	Good fall color
Austrian pine (*Pinus nigra*)	Evergreen tree	Very hardy
Baby's-breath (*Gypsophila elegans*)	Annual	Good in winter arrangements
Beard tongue (*Penstemon hartwegii*)	Annual	Flowers attract hummingbirds
Calliopsis (*Coreopsis tinctoria*)	Annual	Seeds attract birds
Firethorn (*Pyracantha coccinea*)	Evergreen shrub	Berries attract birds
Glossy abelia (*Abelia grandiflora*)	Evergreen shrub	Long bloom period
Juniper (*Juniperus* various)	Evergreen shrub	Very hardy
Livingstone daisy (*Dorotheanthus bellidiformis*)	Annual	Succulent plant
Maidenhair tree (*Ginkgo biloba*)	Deciduous tree	Plant only male tree
Moss rose (*Portulaca grandiflora*)	Annual	Succulent plant; self-seeds
Nasturtium (*Tropaeolum majus*)	Annual	Edible flowers and leaves
Perennial sweet pea (*Lathyrus latifolius*)	Perennial vine	Long bloom period
Rock cotoneaster (*Cotoneaster horizontalis*)	Evergreen shrub	Bright red berries
Russian olive (*Elaeagnus angustifolia*)	Deciduous tree	Fragrant flowers
Spider plant (*Cleome spinosa*)	Annual	Seed capsules good in arrangements
Western redbud (*Cercis occidentalis*)	Deciduous tree	Provides year-round interest

water so much. When you do water, use a soaker hose to cut down on the evaporation problem (see Table 1-8).

Acidity may be a problem in heavy rainfall areas. Many plants will do just fine if the soil is mildly acidic, but will start to fail if it becomes extremely so. Take a soil test, and if the results indicate that your soil needs it, add ground limestone. In the fall, you can dig the soil about a foot deep, spread the lime evenly over the surface, and rake it in (see Table 1-9).

Hardpan soil is often found in the Southwest, where there is an impervious layer of soil near the surface. Man-made hardpan, however, is also found. When your house was built, did the contractors dig out soil for the foundation and dump it where your yard is now? What they probably dug out was subsoil, which is not the best medium in which to grow plants. To compound matters, they probably drove heavy equipment in and out as they were building. When it dries, this can create a dreadful hardpan that roots can't penetrate and water won't drain. The solution again is to add organic matter. Try plowing the soil to a depth of about eighteen inches and mixing the organic matter in. Or go to raised beds. Another solution that involves a lot of back-breaking labor is called *double digging*. It goes like this: Dig out a strip two feet wide and to the depth of your shovel—about a foot. Use a garden fork to thoroughly break up the bottom of the trench you've just made. Incorporate organic material into this trench. Then move to the strip next to the trench and shovel the top foot of soil into the trench you just finished working in, adding more organic material. Repeat this process until the soil you removed from the first trench is used to fill in the last one. Of course, if your hardpan layer is only six inches under the soil, you won't have to dig as far; however, if it is deeper . . . (see Figure 1-12).

If rocks are your problem, one solution is to con the neighborhood kids into thinking that picking rocks and carting them off is a fun way to spend a Saturday afternoon. Remember Tom Sawyer and the fence-painting party? If he can do it, so can you. Again, you can try the raised bed approach or plant in pots and sink them into the ground. This method could create a problem with watering, however. As an alternative solution, many plants will do well in rocky soil (see Table 1-10). This alternative is a whole lot easier on your back than picking rocks.

Do you have swampy soil in which your drainage isn't worth a darn? The first solution that comes to many people's minds is tiling. It's a good solution. However, if you could afford to tile your

TABLE 1-9

Plants for Acidic Areas

NAME	TYPE	COMMENTS
American holly (*Ilex opaca*)	Evergreen tree	Red berries
Bearberry (*Arctostaphylos uva-ursi*)	Evergreen shrub	Ground cover
Camellia (*Camellia* various)	Evergreen shrub	Spring and fall blooming varieties available
Cardinal flower (*Lobelia cardinalis*)	Perennial	Flame red bloom
Chinese holly (*Ilex cornuta*)	Evergreen shrub	Bright red berries
Drooping leucothoe (*Leucothoe fontanesiana*)	Evergreen shrub	Leathery leaves
Heath (*Erica* various)	Evergreen shrub	Attracts bees
Japanese holly (*Ilex crenata*)	Evergreen shrub	Black berries
Japanese privet (*Ligustrum japonicum*)	Evergreen shrub	Fragrant flowers
Leatherleaf viburnum (*Viburnum wrightii*)	Evergreen shrub	Scarlet fruit
Oregon grape (*Mahonia aquifolium*)	Evergreen shrub	Edible blue-black fruit
Rhododendron (*Rhododendron* various)	Evergreen shrub	Some very hardy varieties available
Summer phlox (*Phlox paniculata*)	Perennial	Fragrant flowers
Turk's-cap lily (*Lilium superbum*)	Bulb	Brilliant orange flowers
Violet (*Viola* various)	Perennial	Good ground cover
Wintergreen barberry (*Berberis julianae*)	Evergreen shrub	Dark blue berries

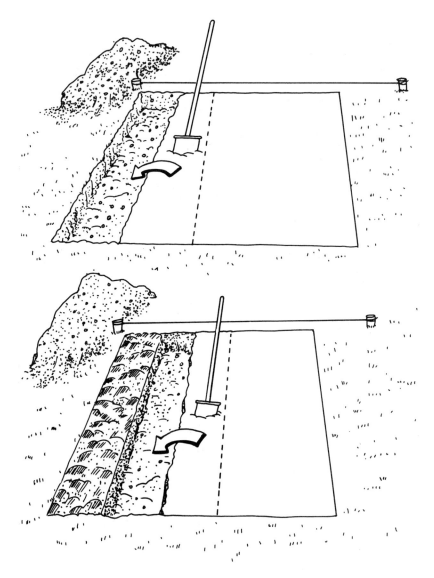

Figure 1-12. Double digging.

yard, you probably wouldn't be reading a book with this title. Tiling is best left to the experts or you may end up accidentally dumping all your excess water on your neighbor's yard or creating an erosion problem in your own back yard. How do you know if

TABLE 1-10

Plants for Rocky Areas

NAME	TYPE	COMMENTS
Angel's hair (*Artemisia schmidtiana*)	Perennial	Makes beautiful silver dome
Aubrieta (*Aubretia deltoidea*)	Perennial	Many colors available
Bar Harbor juniper (*Juniperus horizontalis* 'Bar Harbor')	Evergreen shrub	Turns plum-colored in winter
Basket-of-gold (*Aurinia saxatilis*)	Perennial	Self-seeds
Blue rug juniper (*Juniperus horizontalis* 'Blue Rug')	Evergreen	Good ground cover
Cinquefoil (*Potentilla cinerea*)	Evergreen perennial	Good ground cover
Edging candytuft (*Iberis sempervirens*)	Perennial	Good ground cover
Grevillea (*Grevillea* various)	Evergreen shrub	Drought-tolerant
Hardy aster (*Aster alpinus*)	Perennial	Insect and disease resistant
Lavender (*Lavandula* various)	Evergreen herb	Drought-tolerant
Limber pine (*Pinus flexilis*)	Evergreen tree	Slow grower
Olive (*Olea europaea*)	Evergreen tree	Fruitless varieties available
Ornamental crabapple (*Malus* various)	Deciduous tree	Attracts birds
Rock rose (*Helianthemum nummularium*)	Evergreen perennial	Good ground cover
Round-leaved mallee (*Eucalyptus orbifolia*)	Evergreen	Espaliers well
Soapwort (*Saponaria ocymoides*)	Perennial	Easy from seed
White ironbark (*Eucalyptus leucoxylon*)	Evergreen tree	Fast grower

you have a drainage problem? Dig a hole about two feet deep and fill it with water. If, after twenty-four hours, the water is still in it (or, heaven forbid, has risen), you have poor drainage. Of course, don't try this in the middle of the dry season or you'll probably be certain to find you have excellent drainage. Other than a major operation, the best thing to do with swampy soil is to learn to adapt to it. Many plants will do just fine with wet feet (see Table 1-11). If you want to try others, you'll have to resort once again to raised beds or containers.

To solve any of the problems I've just mentioned, many gardeners will advocate bringing in loads of topsoil. In my experience, this is not an instant answer. First, it's not cheap. Second, you don't always know what you're going to get. In one instance, a friend of mine purchased two truckloads of topsoil. The first load she received had a good, crumbly texture. The second one was worse than the soil she was trying to amend. If you do go the topsoil route, visit the site where the topsoil is dug and see what you're getting. It's also easy to have nasty weeds such as nutgrass, wild morning glory, and quack grass brought in like this. And please realize that you're going to get a dump-truck-size load dropped in your driveway. That's a lot of soil to move around. Just be well prepared with a bottle of liniment after the job is done.

Sometimes the problems you might encounter with your yard are not soil-related. High heat areas can be a nuisance not only in hot summer environments, but anyplace. Even though I live in the Pacific Northwest and our summers are notoriously cool, I have a high heat area on the west side of my white garage which is adjacent to a cement patio. The amount of reflected heat is tremendous, and the little patch of soil is like an oven in July and August. Even my spring bulbs bloom earlier there than in any other part of the yard. If you live in any of the hot summer regions, you'll probably have quite a few "hot spots." For places like these, you'll find quite an array of plants that will not only survive but thrive in the heat (see Table 1-12).

Perhaps you're a city dweller and live in an area with an air-pollution problem. Many plants are very sensitive to the chemicals in automobile exhaust or manufacturing pollutants. But there are others that are extremely tolerant (see Table 1-13). So if you live near large industries or a very busy street, check with the county agent. He will be able to tell you which plants are the most susceptible to pollution. You can tell if a plant is suffering from air

TABLE 1-11

Plants for Wet Areas

NAME	TYPE	COMMENTS
American arborvitae (*Thuja occidentalis*)	Evergreen tree	Makes good hedges
American elderberry (*Sambucus canadensis*)	Deciduous shrub	Edible fruit
Black willow (*Salix nigra*)	Deciduous tree	Very fast-growing
Box elder (*Acer negundo*)	Deciduous tree	Very fast-growing
Bush violet (*Browallia* various)	Annual	Good cut flower
Eastern sycamore (*Platanus occidentalis*)	Deciduous tree	Seed clusters used in arrangements
False dragonhead (*Physostegia virginiana*)	Perennial	Good cut flower
Huckleberry (*Vaccinium* various)	Evergreen shrub	Edible fruit
Iris blue flag (*Iris versicolor*)	Perennial	Will grow in water
Loosestrife (*Lythrum salicaria*)	Perennial	Good cut flower
Monkey flower (*Mimulus* various)	Perennial	Flowers attract birds
Pussy willow (*Salix discolor*)	Deciduous shrub	Easy to grow
Red-osier dogwood (*Cornus sericea*)	Deciduous shrub	Twigs bright red
Royal fern (*Osmunda regalis*)	Deciduous	Very large plant
Shagbark hickory (*Carya ovata*)	Deciduous tree	Edible nuts
Smooth alder (*Alnus rugosa*)	Deciduous tree	Seeds attract birds
Spiderwort (*Tradescantia andersoniana*)	Perennial	Grass-like foliage

TABLE 1-12

Plants for High Heat Areas

NAME	TYPE	COMMENTS
Bamboo (*Bambusa* various)	Grass	May be invasive
California privet (*Ligustrum ovalifolium*)	Deciduous shrub	Good hedge plant
Carolina cherry laurel (*Prunus caroliniana*)	Evergreen shrub	Drought-tolerant
China aster (*Callistephus chinensis*)	Annual	Good cut flower
Climbing rose (*Rosa* various)	Deciduous vine	Some varieties especially fragrant
Edible fig (*Ficus carica*)	Deciduous tree	Needs good drainage
Juniper (*Juniperus* various)	Evergreen shrub	Very hardy
Lavender starflower (*Grewia occidentalis*)	Evergreen shrub	Fast-growing
Marigold (*Tagetes* various)	Annual	Trouble-free
Pearlbush (*Exochorda macrantha*)	Deciduous shrub	Profusion of white flowers
Photinia (*Photinia fraseri*)	Evergreen shrub	Fast growing; good screen
Powderpuff (*Calliandra* various)	Evergreen shrub	Very showy flowers
Rock cotoneaster (*Cotoneaster horizontalis* 'perpusillus')	Deciduous ground cover	Attractive red berries
Southern magnolia (*Magnolia grandiflora*)	Evergreen tree	Needs protection from wind
Wisteria (*Wisteria* various)	Deciduous vine	Needs good drainage
Xylosma (*Xylosma congestum*)	Deciduous shrub	Makes good espalier
Zinnia (*Zinnia* various)	Annual	Watch for mildew problems

TABLE 1-13

Air Pollution-Tolerant Plants

NAME	TYPE	COMMENTS
Arborvitae (*Thuja* various)	Evergreen tree or shrub	Symmetrical shape
Balsam fir (*Abies balsamea*)	Evergreen tree	Slow grower
Canna (*Canna* various)	Tuber	Lends tropical look
Colorado spruce (*Picea pungens*)	Evergreen tree	Very stiff form
Cosmos (*Cosmos* various)	Annual	Self-seeds
European larch (*Larix decidua*)	Deciduous conifer	Good spring and fall color
Juniper (*Juniperus* various)	Evergreen shrub	Very hardy
Patience plant (*Impatiens* various)	Annual	Long bloom period
Periwinkle (*Vinca* various)	Evergreen groundcover	May be invasive
Red oak (*Quercus rubra*)	Deciduous tree	Fast grower
Shasta daisy (*Chrysanthemum superbum*)	Perennial	Drought-resistant
Small-leaved linden (*Tilia cordata*)	Deciduous tree	Fragrant flowers
Spindle tree (*Euonymus* various)	Evergreen shrub	Colorful fruit
Summer cypress (*Kochia scoparia*)	Annual	Dust and wind resistant
Wax begonia (*Begonia semperflorens-cultorum*)	Annuall	Colorful flowers in shady areas
White spruce (*Picea glauca*)	Evergreen tree	Very cold hardy
Yew (*Taxus* various)	Evergreen tree or shrub	Slow grower

pollution if the foliage is spotted, streaked, or bleached or the leaves drop prematurely. Of course, other problems can be the cause of these symptoms, so before blaming a plant's demise on pollution, be sure that insects or disease were not the problem.

Another problem city dwellers often have to put up with is noise. High levels of noise can cut down on your enjoyment of the outdoors. Noise can come from many sources, whether it be automobile traffic, air traffic, sirens, or nearby loud businesses. Whatever the source, evergreen trees and shrubs are the answer to the problem. You'll be amazed at the amount of difference a belt of Norway spruce (*Picea abies*) for example, planted ten to twenty-five feet from the noise source, can make in toning down the amount of sound that reaches your home. Living groundcovers will also absorb more noise than non-living types such as cement or crushed rock (see Table 1-14).

If you invest in property you might run into a situation in which you need to landscape a lot before you sell it. Often you can get quite a bit more money for a house if the lot has already been planted. Or perhaps, you're like I was, and can't wait to get some tall greenery surrounding the unlandscaped house you just bought. In cases like this, you would probably be interested in planting some fairly fast-growing species (see Table 1-15). To me, a tree or shrub is fast growing if it will reach a presentable size in one to four years. Annuals, of course, and many perennials will reach full size in one year. Remember, however, that many fast-growing trees are weak-wooded and therefore will break easily in windy areas or in storms. Also, some fast-growing trees and shrubs get unattractive with old age. So the best idea may be to interplant slow growers among the fast ones. Then when the slower varieties are finally large enough to dominate the landscape, you can remove the fast growers.

Sometimes, especially if you purchase a more established home, the vegetation has grown to such a degree that the entire area is shady. Often the plants that were originally planted were sun lovers, and as the more vigorous ones grew and produced more and more shade, many of these sun lovers became spindly or died out from lack of light. Sometimes these large trees and shrubs are plants of great beauty, and it might be a shame to cut them down. So perhaps it would be wiser to cut down the weak plants and substitute plants that either tolerate or prefer shade (see Figure 1-13 and Table 1-16). While waiting for your trees, shrubs, and perennials to get established, fill in the bare spots with annuals. They'll provide fast growth and an abundance of color (see Figures 1-14, 1-15, and 1-16).

TABLE 1-14

Noise-Screening Plants

NAME	TYPE	COMMENTS
America arborvitae *(Thuja occidentalis)*	Evergreen tree	Very symmetrical growth
Atlas cedar *(Cedrus atlantica)*	Evergreen tree	Slow grower
Chinese juniper *(Juniperus chinensis)*	Evergreen tree	Columnar shape
Common juniper *(Juniperus communis* 'Stricta')	Evergreen tree	Narrow, columnar shape
Deodar cedar *(Cedrus deodara)*	Evergreen tree	Fast grower
Douglas fir *(Pseudotsuga menziesii)*	Evergreen tree	Very soft needles
English yew *(Taxus baccata)*	Evergreen tree	Seeds poisonous
Firethorn *(Pyracantha* various)	Evergreen shrub	Fast grower
Japanese yew *(Taxus cuspidata)*	Evergreen shrub	Slow grower
Norway spruce *(Picea abies)*	Evergreen tree	Fast grower
Oriental arborvitae *(Platycladus orientalis)*	Evergreen shrub	Formal appearance
Ponderosa pine *(Pinus ponderosa)*	Evergreen tree	Can't tolerate extreme heat
Privet *(Ligustrum* various)	Evergreen tree or shrub	Flowers attract bees
Scotch pine *(Pinus sylvestris)*	Evergreen tree	Wind-resistant; very hardy
Spindle tree *(Euonymous japonica)*	Evergreen shrub	Heat-tolerant
Western hemlock *(Tsuga heterophylla)*	Evergreen tree	Fast grower
White fir *(Abies concolor)*	Evergreen tree	Very symmetrical growth

TABLE 1-15

Fast-Growing Plants

NAME	TYPE	COMMENTS
Annual mallow (*Lavatera trimestris*)	Annual	Grows to six feet tall in one season
Black locust (*Robinia pseudoacacia*)	Deciduous	Drought-tolerant
Blue ash (*Fraxinus quadrangulata*)	Deciduous tree	Plant male only
Carpet bugle (*Ajuga reptans*)	Perennial	Ground cover
Castor bean (*Ricinus communis*)	Annual	Poisonous seeds; gives tropical look
Forsythia (*Forsythia intermedia*)	Deciduous shrub	Force branches for indoor bloom
Honey locust (*Gleditsia triacanthos*)	Deciduous tree	Thornless varieties available
Marguerite (*Chrysanthemum frutescens*)	Perennial	Grows to four feet across in one season
Pampas grass (*Cortaderia selloana*)	Evergreen grass	Grows to eight feet tall in one season
Red oak (*Quercus rubra*)	Deciduous tree	Needs much water
River birch (*Betula nigra*)	Deciduous tree	Needs constant moisture
Saxifrage (*Saxifraga rosacea*)	Perennial	Forms spreading cushions
Siberian pea shrub (*Caragana arborescens*)	Deciduous shrub	Very tough; fragrant flowers
Silver maple (*Acer saccharinum*)	Deciduous tree	Insect prone
Weigela (*Weigela florida*)	Deciduous shrub	Coarse-leafed, stiff form
White alder (*Alnus rhombifolia*)	Deciduous tree	Heat- and wind-tolerant
White mulberry (*Morus alba*)	Deciduous tree	Fruitless varieties available

Figure 1-13. Tucking in a small bed of shade-tolerant plants (*Jane Kailing*).

MORE AND MORE INFORMATION

While you're perusing books, magazines, and catalogs making decisions on what type of landscaping you want, you'll see a confusing number of enticing pictures showing a wide variety of landscape plants. It's helpful to make a list of those that particularly appeal to you. Of course, be certain that those you like are hardy in your area. Rhododendrons are fine shrubs, but unless you're an expert it wouldn't be wise to attempt them in southern Arizona. This list will come in especially handy if you're not particularly familiar with plant names and find a plant that isn't in bloom. If you know that the name rings a bell but can't quite remember whether or not you like it, check your list. I even keep a "dislike" list. I write my lists on 3 × 5-inch notecards and carry them in my handbag for easy reference. I find it easier to pass by a plant that is on sale if I know it is on my dislike list. Sometimes, for example, even though the foliage is attractive, I don't particularly care for the bloom. Or, perhaps this plant that looks so innocent and appealing now is actually a notorious self-seeder and will soon take over the garden. It may even be a variety that is very difficult to grow in your area or perhaps is only borderline hardy.

TABLE 1-16

Shade-Tolerant Plants

NAME	TYPE	COMMENTS
Arrowwood (*Viburnum* various)	Deciduous shrub	Fruit attracts birds
Bayberry (*Myrica pensylvanica*)	Evergreen shrub	Leaves fragrant
Begonia (*Begonia* various)	Annual	Great variety of colors
Buffalo currant (*Ribes odoratum*)	Deciduous shrub	Fruit attracts birds
Christmas rose (*Helleborus niger*)	Perennial	Winter blooming
Coleus (*Coleus hybridus*)	Annual	Leaves brightly colored
Coralbells (*Heuchera sanguinea*)	Perennial	Attracts hummingbirds
Creeping lilyturf (*Liriope spicata*)	Perennial	Grass-like leaves
Dwarf mugho pine (*Pinus mugo* 'mugo')	Evergreen shrub	Very hardy
European burning bush (*Euonymus alata*)	Deciduous shrub	Watermelon-color leaves in fall
Fragrant sumac (*Rhus aromatica*)	Deciduous shrub	Fast grower
Hetz blue juniper (*Juniperus chinensis* 'Hetzii')	Evergreen shrub	Blue-gray color
Hicks yew (*Taxus media* 'Hicksii')	Evergreen shrub	Slow grower
Japanese maple (*Acer palmatum*)	Deciduous tree	Good fall and spring color
Patience plant (*Impatiens wallerana*)	Annual	Good for color
Shadbush (*Amelanchier* various)	Deciduous tree	Fruit attracts birds
Witch hazel (*Hamamelis* various)	Deciduous tree	Fragrant winter flowers

Figures 1-14, 1-15, 1-16. Using annuals as fill-ins (*Jane Kailing*).

For good reason, much is mentioned about hardiness in landscaping books. It is one of the most important factors in considering a plant for your yard. It won't do me any good to pine (no pun intended) over the fantastically fragrant Arabian jasmine (*Jasminum sambac*), because unless I put it in a greenhouse, it won't grow outside in my climatic zone. So before you get your heart set on a particular plant, study the United States Department of Agriculture Plant Hardiness Zone Map and determine in which zone you live (see Figure 1-17).

Often, books dealing with plants indicate the zones in which the plants will live—but here's a word of warning. Some books have different systems for numbering or lettering the zones than that of the United States Department of Agriculture. When you look at a book, be certain to determine that if, according to the United States Department of Agriculture map, you live in zone 7, for instance, the authors of that book also consider your location zone 7. If not, check to see which zone you are in according to their system and then choose plants accordingly.

And please try not to plant problems. Some species may have particular problems that call for more intensive care than you want to give. Do you know how often roses need to be sprayed to keep them in top shape? In some parts of the country, a plant may have more problems than in others. Where I live, the poor European white birch (*Betula pendula*) has a multitude of enemies— leaf miner, birch borer, spider mite, and aphid. I love the tree, but I won't grow one because of these problems. Other plants that could cause difficulties include mulberry (*Morus* various) and female maidenhair tree (*Gingko biloba*), which produce messy fruit; sweet gum (*Liquidambar* various), which has spiny fruit nicknamed "gumballs" that kids love to throw; poplar (*Populus* various) and mimosa (*Albizia julibrissin*) have seeds, which will sprout all over your flower beds; sumac (*Rhus* various), which tends to produce suckers, especially if the roots are disturbed; and willow (*Salix* various) has roots, which are invasive and tend to clog nearby sewers. But each of these plants works well in the right place; just be aware of their shortcomings and plant them accordingly.

The garden section of your local newspaper is an excellent source of information because it is regional and deals with problems, "do's" and "don'ts," and varieties that are endemic to your area. I moved from the Midwest to the Pacific Northwest and found the local paper's gardening section extremely useful in

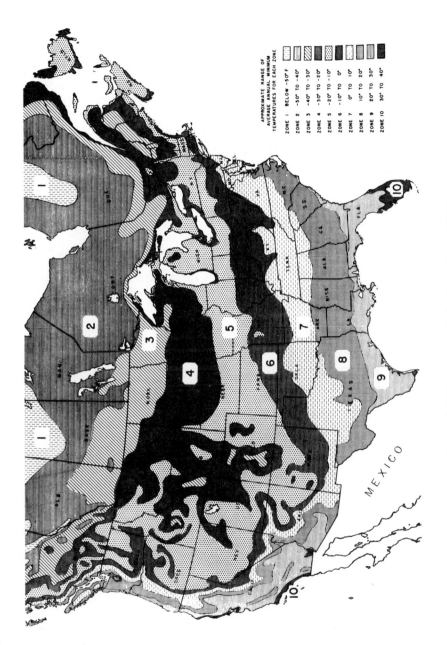

Figure 1-17. The zones of plant hardiness (*USDA*).

helping me learn what the standard practices are. I had no idea how to handle plants such as azaleas, heathers, and andromedas. Some plants that we treated like annuals in Wisconsin are perennials in Oregon.

Check your local library to see if there is a regional gardening book published for your area. An excellent one on the Pacific Northwest is *Sunset New Western Garden Book* (Menlo Park, CA: Lane Publishing Company, 1981). I would recommend it for either the novice or the advanced gardener.

There seem to be books written on gardening in any section of the country you can name. Here are a few others:

A Southern Garden: A Handbook for the Middle South
Elizabeth Lawrence
University of North Carolina Press, 1967

Florida Gardening Month by Month
Nixon Smiley
University of Miami Press, 1980

Fred Heutte's Gardening in the Temperate Zone
Frederic Heutte
Donning Company, 1977

Garden Book for Houston and the Gulf Coast
River Oaks Garden Club, ed.
Pacesetter Press, 1975

Gardening from the Merrimack to the Kennebec: A Personal Approach to Growing Flowers, Herbs, Fruits & Vegetables
Piscatague Gardening Club, compiled by
Heritage Books, 1978

Gardening in the Upper Midwest
Leon Snyder
University of Minnesota Press, 1978

Gardening on the Eastern Seashore
Marilyn R. Schmidt
Barnegat, 1982

Rocky Mountain Horticulture
George W. Kelly
Pruett, 1967

Southwest Gardening
Rosalie Doolittle & Harriet Tiedebohl
University of New Mexico Press, 1967

The Pacific Gardener
A.R. Willis
Superior Pub., 1976

Trees & Shrubs for Northern Gardens
Leon C. Snyder
University of Minnesota Press, 1980

Tropical Gardening Along the Gulf Coast
Gerald Arp
Pacesetter Press, 1978

Also take a look at periodicals such as *Flower and Garden, Horticulture, Organic Gardening,* and the like. You can get dozens of tips from them.

Seed catalogs can be an enjoyable diversion on a cold or rainy day. Some of the better catalogs not only list the basics about the plant but also give some of its cultural requirements. Most seed companies advertise in gardening periodicals, which are available in the local library. For instance, *Organic Gardening* mentions in its January 1982 issue that if you send a self-addressed, stamped envelope, you will receive a list of reputable seed, bulb, and nursery companies with information on their specialties and how to receive their catalogs.

The Mailorder Association of Nurserymen also has a consumer guide called *The Complete Guide to Gardening by Mail.* It has over 6,000 separate listings for available plants and plant-related items. All it takes to receive it is a self-addressed, stamped envelope and thirty-seven cents postage. Send the envelope to the Mailorder Association of Nurserymen, Inc., 210 Cartwright Boulevard, Massapequa Park, New York 11762.

Now that you have some ideas about the results you want and have identified some plants you like, you can start another activity. You can even kill two birds with one stone by getting great exercise and good ideas too. Take a walk in your own neighborhood or find an area that has landscaping that appeals to you and walk there. If you are lucky enough to have floral gardens or an arboretum in a nearby park, check that out too. Take notes on what you like and what you don't. These are idea walks.

A GOLD MINE IN THE ADS

Next, check out the local shoppers' guides. In the town where I live a free weekly guide published by a grocery store is available. Not only is it free, it offers a free advertisement service too. During the growing season, a person will usually find several advertisements for excess plants that are placed by people who want to give the plants away or sell them at a nominal price. The people who place these advertisements are generally plant lovers who don't have the heart to throw away their extras. It's a good idea to call, even if you don't want what they have. You can say that you aren't exactly sure what the plant they have looks like and ask for a description. Then you can say that you don't have any place for that particular type and ask if there are any other plants they might be interested in sharing. Tell the advertiser you're just learning to garden and that you just bought a house with no landscaping whatsoever. Say anything just to get a response. Ask questions about which plants do best in certain situations, what to do about insects, etc. Usually the advertisers will be flattered that you value their opinion so highly. If you are invited to get some plants, be sure to pay a compliment on their landscaping, even if it's not exactly your favorite style (only if it's well done, of course). Or if the landscaping is atrocious, say something nice about the roses, or dahlias, or tulips. You'd be surprised at what you can glean with this technique. The advertisements may mention two rose bushes, but if you play your cards right you can come home with a trunkful of other assorted plants, many of them free.

Watch out for some advertisements, however. In a supplemental section of our Sunday paper, I've noticed several unbelievable ads. One advertised a plant that would grow quickly to a "large size," bloom all year, and miracle of miracles, deodorize an entire room—all this for a mere $4.98 plus postage. Naturally, I wondered what this fantastic plant could be. I couldn't identify it from the "artist's rendition," but after searching the fine print I saw *Pelargonium tomentosum* in teeny letters. Here's where knowing the scientific names came in handy. It was a peppermint-scented geranium—no exotic wonder plant at all. If I wanted one, I could get a cutting from a friend or even purchase a plant at a nursery for a lot less money.

Then there was the advertisement for the fast-growing tree that would reach fifty feet in only a few years. It was supposed to have lovely, unusual green flowers and be extremely tough. Again, I checked the small print and found *Ailanthus altissima*. That's the tree-of-heaven and, yes, it is a fast grower. What the advertisement failed to mention is that it suckers profusely, seeds itself all over the place, is weak-wooded, and has very inconspicuous flowers. The advertisers were right about it surviving under adverse conditions, however. In hot, droughty areas it survives where others won't, but I sure wouldn't want one where I live. Buyer beware.

NOW I'VE GOT 'EM, WHAT DO I DO WITH 'EM?

Be sure to keep all your plants moist from the time they're dug until you plant them. Keeping them moist, however, does not mean standing the root ball in water as one of my friends did. She had dug some plants and called to ask if I wanted them. Because I was busy until the next day, I asked her to keep them moist and in the shade until I could come to get them. When I arrived to pick them up, I found that she had put them, soil and all, into a bucket full of water. Thankfully, I got them out in time, and they did not perish. Putting the plants in a bucket and sprinkling the roots would have been adequate. Standing a plant in water with a lot of soil around its roots cuts down the oxygen in the soil and the plant will suffocate. Remember, plants need to breathe, too.

Another time, I got some cuttings of a hardy fuschia from a woman who advertised free calla lilies. She and I talked after she had taken the cuttings, and by the time I got them home the fuschias were totally wilted. I tried to revive them by putting them in water for a few hours, but even that didn't work. Had I taken the precaution of wrapping the cuttings in a wet paper towel or even putting them in a plastic bag, I might have some fuschias today.

Also, when you're transferring plants, especially larger ones, please don't put them in the back of a pickup without some protection. Even if you drive slowly, they will probably get windburned or dessicated if it's hot. If the plants are small, cover them with a box. If they're large, place a large plastic garbage bag over the leaves and tie it loosely around the trunk or base. Then drive slowly so the bag doesn't whip the plant to death.

Remember your like and dislike list when you're in the position to get free plants. Learn to say no to plants you don't like or that don't fit into your landscape plans. I now find myself digging out plants that I knew I didn't care for when I got them just because I couldn't say no to the generous person who offered them to me. It may be awkward to explain why all the free foxgloves are not in your garden if the donor happens to visit. If you don't like a plant, don't take it. If you have a hard time turning people down, take the plant with the understanding that it is for a friend of yours who loves that particular kind. Then either find a friend who wants it or throw it away. Either way, the donor won't expect to see it on a future visit.

2

Ask
and
You Shall Receive

When you take walks, you will probably run into people working in their yards. Always stop and chat. Most people who have nice yards are highly complimented to have someone notice and are more than happy to answer questions, give advice, and even give you plants. Yes, I said *give* you plants. One comment that I find especially useful in acquiring plants by this method is to say, "My, that's a lovely plant. Would you mind telling me what it is so I can go to a nursery and buy one?" Unless the person has no heart at all, there is only one other one like it in the United States, or you have taken a liking to a thirty-foot Scotch pine (*Pinus sylvestris*), chances are you'll get a sample or a promise of seeds or cuttings in the future. This works especially well in the spring or fall when people are thinning out or transplanting and have more than they know what to do with. I usually carry a few assorted sizes of plastic bags, which are useful for carrying plants so they don't dry out and go into shock. It's amazing how I can come up with reasons for "just happening" to have bags in my pocket. If you're walking a dog, the idea that you might pick up its droppings will probably endear you to the person with a well-landscaped yard. If you have a little dog and feel the need to carry big baggies, it's up to you . . . figure out your own answer. The plastic bags in the produce section of the grocery store are the perfect size. So stash away all those bags in which you get your broccoli, radishes, and tomatoes.

As you are taking your walks, peer up and down alleys for cast-off plants. You'd be surprised at what goodies people will throw out. My husband once brought me a small tree peony (*Paeonia* various) that he had found discarded. For those of you who are not familiar with them, they're a bit on the expensive side. Named varieties can go upwards of ten dollars each.

NEIGHBORHOOD WATCH

If you've noticed a house for sale with a yard that at one time had beautiful landscaping but has been neglected, keep an eye on it. When the new owners move in, they will probably be over-whelmed by the work ahead of them, both inside and outside the house. Watch for the time they start on the yard work. Many plants, when left on their own for a while, will reproduce and reproduce until they are too crowded. This results in reduced flower size or diminished numbers. Plants such as lily-of-the-val-ley (*Convallaria majalis*), dahlia (*Dahlia* various), iris (*Iris* vari-ous), chrysanthemum (*Chrysanthemum* various), and most flowering bulbs, to name a few, especially have this problem. In a situation like this, it is really to the new owners' advantage to dig up and divide plants. You would be doing a good deed by giving this information. Of course, you should mention that if they don't know what to do with the extra divisions, you'd be happy to take them off their hands. Or, if they seem unsure about the correct method to divide their plants, volunteer to show them. How could someone be so cold-hearted that they would not share with you after you've been so helpful? This is where knowing how to divide plants correctly comes in handy. I'll talk about the ways to do this in Chapter 7, "The Maternity Ward."

I find more flower bulbs discarded than anything else. The nice thing about bulbs is that they can lie out of the soil for quite a long time and still come up and flower the next year if they are taken care of correctly. I'll go into how to do that in Chapter 6, "The Infirmary."

The only problem with picking bulbs out of throwaway piles is that it's rather embarrassing to have to go to the owner's house and ask if he could kindly identify the pilfered bulb you "found" in the alley. I may be gutsy, but even *I* couldn't handle this situation. Most often when this happens, I'll just go ahead and plant the bulb. Usually, the bigger the bulb, the bigger the plant, so it's fairly simple to tell where to place it in the flower bed. So far, I haven't had any major problems using this method except for some clashing colors. When this happens, I just dig out the offending color and move it. If you don't like this method, you can always plant the bulbs in an unobtrusive place for the first year until they have bloomed and you know what you have.

Since many bulbs, corms, tubers, and such are quite dif-ferent in appearance, I've included Figure 2-1a, b, and c to help you distinguish one from another. Unfortunately, just because you can identify the bulb you found as a daffodil, you'll still have no idea which variety it is—and there are hundreds of them. You'll just have to plant it, wait, and see.

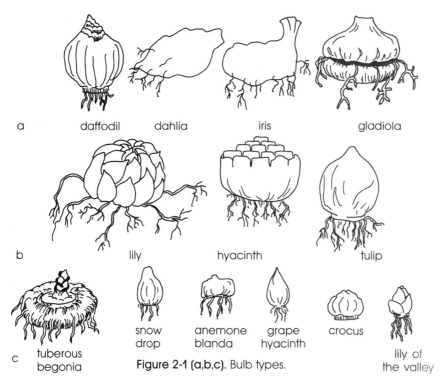

a daffodil dahlia iris gladiola

b lily hyacinth tulip

c tuberous begonia

snow drop

anemone blanda

grape hyacinth

crocus

lily of the valley

Figure 2-1 (a,b,c). Bulb types.

Many gardeners don't divide clumps of the smaller bulbs such as crocus (*Crocus* various), snowdrop (*Galanthus* various), grape hyacinth (*Muscari* various), windflower (*Anenome* various), squill (*Scilla* various), or ornamental onion (*Allium* various), so you are not as likely to run into them in an alley. Fortunately, these are very inexpensive bulbs to buy (especially wholesale) and they also multiply quickly, so with the outlay of a few dollars you'll be able to add a lot of variety to your landscaping. Of course, because of these plants' tendency to populate an area quickly, if you know someone who has these types of bulbs, he or she probably wouldn't mind digging a few to share with you.

Something else to watch for when taking walks is lily plants. Some species of hardy garden lilies (*Lilium* various) produce aerial bulbils on the leaf axils, where the stem and leaf join. These are actually little baby bulbs. Usually you'll find quite a few green or purplish black bulbils. Pick off the largest ones and plant them one inch deep in summer or early fall. The first year you will get only foliage, but usually plants will blossom during the second year. You can also use this method with gladiolus (*Gladiolus* various), although you'll have to wait until the corms are dug to get the little cormels. They are produced right on the mother corm. So if you spot some gladiolus that you would like to have in your yard, knock on the owner's door and ask if you can have a few cormels when it comes time to dig the plants. Perhaps you can offer to trade a plant or two that you have if the owner appears reluctant.

One minor problem I ran into was entirely my own fault. I had just finished reading about tuberous begonias in an excellent article with unbelievable color pictures. Shortly thereafter, while on a walk, I happened upon a pile of discarded tubers and decided that they just *had* to be begonias. I carefully took them home, potted them up, and watered them, and then waited impatiently for the first sign of green. Naturally, the first tiny leaves looked just like begonias. I was ecstatic. If you've ever priced begonia tubers, you'll know why. I babied those "begonias" and catered to them. Since I found them fairly late in the season, I wasn't sure if they were going to bloom before frost—but I didn't care. I planned just where I would plant them the following spring to show them off to their full advantage.

Being plant watchers, my husband and I went to the state fair to check out the floral displays. When we came to the tuberous begonias, my husband commented that the leaves didn't look like the ones on the plants we had. In my infinite widsom, I informed him that ours probably were a different variety and so had different leaves. Secretly I thought that ours would be a very unusual type and perhaps would even have exotically marked flowers. When we got home, we had to pass the "begonias" on the way into the house. My husband stopped to examine the leaves. Again he had the nerve to mention that they really didn't resemble begonia leaves and even pointed out their dissimilarities. I remained staunch in my views and would not even consider the thought that I might have imposters on my hands. Inside, however, I was beginning to have doubts. While he busied himself in the house, I sneaked outside to look at them again. This time I looked closer than ever before and, to my dismay, found that the petioles (the stems of the leaves) looked suspiciously like—I can barely bring myself to say it—rhubarb! My precious treasures were rhubarb plants! I won't even describe the pain I went through having to tell my husband what they really were. Let it suffice to say that he had a very smug look on his face, although I do have to give him credit for not saying "I told you so." I'm sure that I would have been much more cautious about assuming what they were had I not just read the article on tuberous begonias. I have learned a lesson. Now would anybody like to trade two dozen healthy rhubarb plants for a tuberous begonia? Maybe I should write a book entitled *Using Rhubarb in the Home Landscape.*

TAKE THE PLUNGE

Depending on how much soil is around their roots, succulents and some woody plants, like bulbs, can last an amazing length of time out of the ground. If on a walk you happen to pick up some plants that are looking pretty wilted and you're not sure if they'll make it, take them home and remove all the dry soil from around their roots. Then plunge the roots and half the stem into cool water in a shady place for a few hours. Remove any flowers that are on the plant. Don't put the plants in water with lots of soil still on their roots and don't leave them there for more than half a day. If the tops don't perk up, the roots are not capable of getting the water to them. The leaves don't have to look as if they were just brought from a florist, but you should notice a difference. Look at the roots, too. If they look shrively, like the carrot you forgot in the vegetable crisper for three months, chances are the plant won't make it. But do give it a chance anyway by using the water method. I've been amazed at the comebacks of some of the sickly looking specimens I've dragged home. If the soil around the roots of the plant is somewhat moist, just pot it, place it in the shade, and water it well. Later, after it makes a comeback, you can add it to your landscape. Identifying plants that come from throwaway piles is easier than identifying bulbs. Usually, if I don't know what I have, it's back to the library for me. With all the color pictures and excellent descriptions available, it's not hard to figure out what plant it is.

Since most of the plants you'll be acquiring will come without pots and you might prefer to place the plants in pots until you decide if they're keepers, it's also a good idea to look for discarded pots. Usually, the clay type are the ones most frequently discarded. These are fine as temporary homes for your orphans. Since most people have a tendency to overwater and clay pots are more porous than plastic, they allow the plants to breathe. Occasionally, you'll find a stack of clay pots that has stuck together. While no amount of prying will get the pots apart without breaking at least a few, they will separate easily if they are soaked in water for a while. Of course, if you're into recycling, any number of items—from large tin cans to milk jugs—can serve as pots. Just remember to punch holes in the bottoms and sides of these home-made pots to prevent drowning your finds. Why punch holes in the sides, you ask? If you punch holes only in the bottom and the container sits flat on the ground, it's harder for the water to get out. It meets no resistance on the sides, so there's less chance of drowning your plant.

SPREAD THE WORD

Besides walking and looking and asking, be sure to let all your friends and neighbors know that you're on the lookout for plants. If you know any real estate agents, put them at the head of your list. They often know before anyone else that a house is being torn down or moved to make way for a parking lot or super-market. This is a bonanza for you because the people tearing down the house often won't care about the landscape. Usually the plants are well-established and sometimes the older, harder-to-get varieties. Older roses, for example, may be much more fragrant than some of the newer varieties. You'll find that old-fashioned sweet peas (*Lathyrus odoratus*) and flowering tobacco (*Nicotiana sylvestris*) have a sweeter scent, too.

Think about joining a garden club. Even if you don't join, at least plan to visit a few. Members usually are very friendly to neophytes and are willing to share all their gardening tips. Let them know that you're interested in acquiring starts and you'll be amazed at how quickly word will get around. You can get the names of local clubs from the local library or check the "Club News" section of your newspaper. Many clubs have a plant exchange at their meetings, so it's a good idea to find out ahead of time if you should bring a plant. You can get some fantastic specimens this way as long-time members try to outdo each other. Some groups even give away a plant as a door prize, so if you're one of those people who always win the drawings, you might walk away from a meeting with several additions to your garden.

Try running an advertisement in a weekly shopper. I usually use a small local paper because it's generally less expensive and doesn't cover such a large geographic area. With the cost of gas, it doesn't pay to get free plants if you have to drive fifty miles one way to get them. I've found that an advertisement that is worded a little differently gets more attention and thus more results. Try one that starts out with the word "HELP!" Most people will be curious enough to read at least the first line, so hit them up right away with what you're looking for. Also, be sure to state that you are willing to come and dig up plants—carefully, of course. If a person answers your advertisement and says he has a boxwood that he wants to get rid of and you wouldn't be caught dead with one in your yard, for heaven's sake don't mention your dislike. Put a smile in your voice and inform him that unfortunately you have no place in your landscape plans for a boxwood. Sound very regretful. Then ask if he has anything else with which he might be willing to part. Say you would even be interested in divisions, cuttings, or seeds. Instead of just throwing their plants out, people who care enough to answer an advertisement like yours are generally the type who are willing to share their knowledge and greenery with you.

3

Volunteer
and
You Shall Receive

Some time ago, while perusing our paper's garden section, I noticed a small article describing the activities of a group of local volunteer gardeners. They were working on an historic house's garden and were re-creating it as it had been in the 1890s. I'm fond of old-fashioned plants and gardens, so the idea intrigued me. I called the phone number included at the end of the article to find out more about the group. In talking to the one in charge, I found out that the group worked one morning a week for three to four hours. I promptly decided I could afford that much time, and so on their next scheduled workday I arrrived with shovel in hand. That was the beginning of a very educational experience. I learned everything from what varieties were used "way back when" to the vast difference between yesterday and today's ideas of landscaping. Of course, aside from learning, I also met several nice people who were not only knowledgeable, but who were also interested in trading plants. An extra bonus came about because part of our work was to remove any "newer" plants that did not conform to the old garden plan. Some were transplanted to another area, but others, because there were so many, were discarded—or were given to one of the volunteers. Guess who was there with her hand out?

Adjacent to the historic house was a city park. Another group had undertaken a project there that involved children in vegetable gardening. Unfortunately, about halfway through the season they lost momentum and the garden became neglected and overgrown with weeds. The plants, however, had had enough care to produce, but there was no one to harvest. After asking permission of the city gardener, I harvested some of the vegetables. From then on, I didn't have to be concerned about taking a lunch along when I worked in the historical garden; I only had to walk over to the vegetable plot to find all the fresh vegetables I could eat. And they were all organically grown—an extra bonus. I even noticed the city gardener there eating lunch, a warm tomato in one hand and a fresh cucumber in the other.

Did I hear someone say, "That's all well and good, but I work forty hours a week and don't have any time to volunteer"? At one time, I did too—but I still found the time. How? By using my lunch hours. Instead of going shopping, eating out, or sitting around talking, I used that time to volunteer at a garden. It took me fifteen minutes to walk there and back, which left me forty-five minutes to work. And yes, I was nicely dressed, but I still managed to do some of the chores. I pruned and watered and did a bit of light weeding. I went twice a week and concluded that I not only gained many plants, but I lost some weight by skimping on lunch and getting mild exercise. I ate a carton of yogurt on the way to the garden and a piece of fruit on the way back to work. Unfortunately, there wasn't a nearby vegetable garden to raid. By my calculations, each week, for working about two hours, I took home an average of twenty dollars' worth of plants. That means, in effect, I was getting ten dollars an hour. Not a bad wage for manual labor.

If there are no historic sites nearby, you'll find many other places that can use volunteer help. Governmental agencies whose budgets have been cut back are especially appreciative. It seems that gardening and landscaping positions are often the first to be cut out, so many agencies are working with skeleton crews and would probably jump at the chance to get some help. Don't wait as I did for an article to appear in the newspaper requesting volunteers. Find an area that has interesting landscaping, determine who takes care of it, and go to the person. Try to find the one who is actually out there working on the grounds, not the person sitting behind a desk pushing papers. He may not be totally apprised of the situation in the field, so he probably would be more apt to say no. If you go to the supervisor of the work crew and demonstrate your sincerity, he or she may want your help and figure out a way to get approval for you. Let the supervisor handle the paper pusher.

Some places you might look into would be city and state park departments, arboretums, civic gardens, government buildings, children's programs, and cemeteries. Don't laugh—many cemeteries look more like parks than some of the parks I've seen. And don't give up. If you're turned down at one place, go to another. Yes, going to them is better than calling, unless you know for sure that they're looking for volunteers. It's a good idea to give the impression that you've had some experience so they won't think they're starting out with someone completely green. Some places provide training "their way," while others don't want to bother.

FERTILIZE YOUR MIND

If you have no background in gardening but would like some, call the county extension office and ask if a Master Gardener Program is offered. The phone number will be in the white pages of the directory under the county in which you live. This class is currently being offered in over thirty states. In Oregon, there are sixty hours of classroom work covering subjects such as soils, fertilizers, and care of grass, vegetables, fruit trees, houseplants, and ornamentals. The classes are taught by a variety of local experts and are geared toward the novice. You need not have an extensive background in gardening to keep up with the instructor. All you need is a desire to learn and an avid interest in gardening. A definite benefit is that this class is free. What it does cost is time. My class met for six hours once a week for ten weeks. After the sessions are finished, you are expected to volunteer sixty hours of your time as payment. These hours can include anything from answering other gardeners' questions at the state fair (you get a free pass to get in) or a garden center to writing gardening articles and giving speeches at garden clubs. You perform whatever task you feel most comfortable with. All in all, I found it one of the most worthwhile classes I've ever taken. What I liked best was that the information was specific to this area. I had received a degree in horticulture, but it was from the Midwest and so many of the practices that I learned in those classes did not apply to this part of the country. The soils, insects, weather, and just about every other gardening variable are different in the Northwest. The instructors were extremely knowledgeable and even answered questions after class about our personal gardens. I've saved a considerable amount of time and money by knowing the best time to apply fertilizers, how much to use, which kind of pesticides work the best (and which are the safest), and which varieties are particularly suited to this climate. Again, I met delightful people who had the same interests as I. I even met a woman who is as much of a scrounger as I am. Needless to say, we did some heavy trading.

Another program offered in our area is a "sister" to the Master Gardener Program. It's called Master Food Preserving and works on the same principle. If you are interested in vegetable or fruit gardening and want to know the latest techniques and shortcuts in canning, freezing, drying, and so on, this is the class for you. Again, call the county extension office for details.

If no similar programs are offered in your area, call local colleges or universities to determine what types of classes are offered. Often evening adult classes will be offered on gardening subjects. Generally, these are inexpensive and well worth the time. I've even taken one-day seminars on everything from pruning fruit trees to planting a terrarium. Or, you might find that some of the local nurseries or greenhouses offer classes for a nominal fee. Through a nursery, I took a class on landscape design and another on plant propagation. Each was excellent. Even if you don't learn as much as you expected, the people you meet and the plant starts you get will make the effort worthwhile. Not only that, but you will become acquainted with experts in the field. This is great when you have a question or problem. I know that when a nursery offers classes the object is to get you to buy from them. I usually don't (unless there's a *big* sale, in which case the class is usually the first to hear about it) and I don't feel guilty.

FAIR'S FAIR GAME

Another excellent place to volunteer is at county or state fairs. At our state fair, the majority of the floral garden area is kept up by volunteers. Find out if the fair nearest you uses volunteers, then ask if you may help in your particular area of interest. Or, if you have an area that you would *like* to know more about, request that job. Some fairs have budgets large enough to be able to hire all the full-time help they need, but I've observed that these are few and far between. Our state fair floral department has a program called "adopt-a-garden." A volunteer chooses any garden he or she is interested in (rose, herb, perennial, lily, annual, everlasting, etc.) and then is responsible for keeping up that area. This can include planning, planting, fertilizing, watering, pinching, or weeding. It's excellent hands-on experience. If you are unsure of your abilities, don't let that deter you. There will always be people in charge who have a background in gardening and who will supervise you. If you have any questions or problems, they will be there to assist you.

If, perchance, you're looking for a job, a fair is a good place to volunteer. Of course, hard work is a must. As fair time approaches, many landscapers, florists, and growers will be putting up their displays. You will probably work side by side with them and have the opportunity to make friends with some. Admire their work, ask questions, and let them know you're available. You never know when something may pop up. After the fair is over, volunteer to help tear down their displays. You could even ask if they would give you a call if any positions are available in the near future. It's always easier to land a position if the person responsible for hiring is familiar with you and your work. You would certainly have the jump on anyone who simply fills out an application. Nothing is as impersonal as an application form. You're not looking for work? Help anyway and I'll bet you get a free plant or two at the end, or perhaps make a special deal.

While you're volunteering at the fair, keep your eyes open for throwaways. I was amazed at what some of the landscapers and other exhibitors threw out. I found a whole dumpster full of large pots and plastic flats. It didn't take me long to load my car. And after the fair was over, I found some potted shrubs that had been thrown away. Granted, they were a little sorry looking, but a bit of extra love and care took care of that problem. A friend of mine who had volunteered to help inside the floral building with the cut flower displays found several dried arrangements in a wastebasket at the end of the fair. Perhaps the exhibitor didn't win a prize and was disgusted with her efforts. For whatever reason, they were thrown away and are now gracing my friend's dining-room table and buffet.

Volunteering doesn't always have to mean driving clear across town or spending all day away from home. For instance, before I moved to the Northwest, I had a neighbor who liked to camp on weekends. In Arkansas even two days without water in the heat of the summer is too much for many plants. So I volunteered to water my friend's garden on the weekends when he was gone. What did I get in return? As many vegetables as I could eat. That was a bonanza for me since I didn't have a yard big enough for a sizable vegetable garden. My vegetables were tucked in among the ornamentals. If you have all the vegetables you want, perhaps you could exchange watering for a division of that special plant in his or her yard that you've been eyeing. Of course, you could just be a nice neighbor and do it for nothing. Then perhaps later when your friend has something you would like a start of you would feel more comfortable asking for a piece because in effect he or she "owes you one."

At another time I performed a similar service and received free vegetable starts. That was before I became interested in starting my own seeds, so the neighbor's starts were always welcome.

Once I helped an older neighbor by pruning her apple tree and hauling away the branches. For that she gave me some divisions of several very old-fashioned plants that had been in her yard for years and years. Besides that, at harvest time, she brought me a jar of apple butter. Often in situations like these, people will offer to pay me something. I never take money but am not shy to tell them what in their yard I am interested in. It never seems to dawn on people that they can barter plants for work.

In the next chapter, I will discuss how to obtain wholesale catalogs and order from them. This is a good area in which to volunteer a service to your gardening friends. In one catalog, I noticed that a 6 percent discount was allowed if the order exceeded $200. I called my friends and volunteered to share the catalog with them in order to make a larger order. Because of the wholesale prices, most of them ordered and all I had to do for the discount was collect the money and distribute the plants when they came. It worked out very well, and I've been doing it on a yearly basis ever since, substituting new gardeners I meet along the way for ones who have ordered their limits.

Sometimes opportunities repeat themselves; other times once-in-a-lifetime deals appear and you have to act quickly. I read in the paper that a road a block away from my home was going to be widened. The article even mentioned how many feet were going to be taken from yards on each side of the road. Since much of the property involved businesses, I concluded that most would not bother to take out and replant anything that would have to be removed during the widening project. So I took a walk along the road, notebook in hand, and jotted down the plants that interested me. When the work crews arrived, I was ready for them. The deal I made with the foreman was that in exchange for cake or cookies once or twice a week, he would let me know when his crews were going to tear up a section that involved some desirable plants. The workers even helped me dig some of the larger plants. I got what I wanted and they got their tummies filled.

ONE GOOD TURN DESERVES ANOTHER

The local Chamber of Commerce has a program whereby just before Christmas and Easter the local shopping centers donate their display poinsettias and Easter lilies to senior centers and rest homes. I volunteered to deliver a carload of these plants. The joy on the people's faces was worth the time in itself, but I also found a sweet lady who insisted I take a cutting of one of her prize African violets, a hybrid she had created herself, in exchange for the poinsettia I had brought her. The woman has since passed away, but I still have the violet and give a cutting to anyone who wants one.

Another time I became civic-minded and volunteered to help at a city-wide "Dump Day." On this day, the city set up huge dumpsters in various locations for people to get rid of anything they wanted (except cranky husbands or obnoxious kids). I volunteered to stand at the entrance and guide the people to the correct dumpsters (separate ones were for metals, paper, etc.). As they came in, my job was to ask what it was they were dumping. Most of the stuff was junk, but if it was something I could use, I asked if I might have it instead of its being dumped. Permission was almost always granted. I came away with boxes of pots and canning jars and an assortment of potted plants ranging in health from terribly sick to excellent. To top that off, I got a lawn chair, a doghouse, and several trashcans that I later made into compost cans. In the process, I helped clean up my community.

If you know of any small nurseries or greenhouses that are run by just a few people, you might volunteer to help them out during their busy season. I know of one place that has a volunteer clerk one day a week. Of course, if this volunteer spies a plant that is on her want list, she can usually manage to get a few cuttings or purchase it for a song. If you've got any background in gardening, volunteer to help pinch or prune plants—then you can get all the cuttings you want. Maybe you could make a deal up front to have any wages in plant material.

There are so many facets to volunteering that I'm certain you can find at least one to fit your time frame and life style. Besides all the obvious advantages, you get a good feeling in your heart from doing something nice for someone.

4

Going Once, Going Twice— Sales and Auctions

there's a whole bunch more in the car...and they were all *half price!*

It's a good idea to haunt local nurseries and let them know you're landscaping your yard. You might find salespeople at these places who are very friendly and informative and don't mind "having their brains picked" by someone who very probably will buy only their sale items. Occasionally, though, a staff member may be uncooperative almost to the point of hostility if he or she feels you are a bargain hunter and usually won't buy. By the process of trial and error, I've come to know which places and which salespeople to go to when I need information and don't want to end up feeling guilty about taking their time. I also know which nurseries have the best sales. So when you talk with salespeople, be sure to find out when their sales are held and where they're advertised so you can keep a lookout for them. Sometimes they'll have a mailing list of their "preferred customers" who get a notice in the mail even before the ads come out in the paper. This gives you a jump on almost everyone else and you get the "pick of the litter," so to speak. Just a request to be on the list may be sufficient. Other times, it may be necessary to buy something; or begging and pleading could do the trick. However, it is rarely necessary to go to the extent of tears.

While you're checking out nursery sales, see if there is a landscape designer on their staff to answer questions and help people with their problems. Before you dash to the person behind the drawing board, however, find out if the service holds an obligation. Many times, routine questions and simple landscape planning hints are free of charge. If, however, you are interested in a complete landscape plan, there is usually a fee for the drawings. If you have a particularly troublesome yard (a swamp behind your garage, or terrain reminiscent of a roller coaster), you might find their services (and charges) worthwhile. In the majority of troublesome cases, the landscape designer will pay a visit to the problem area to get first-hand information before making any major suggestions. If this happens to you, have a list of questions already prepared. Every minute the designer is on your property should be filled with the gathering of information. After all, you're paying for his or her time, so you should get your money's worth.

THE OLD "SEASONAL GREENHOUSE" TRICK

One idea that's worth a try concerns seasonal greenhouses. In some climates, it's uneconomical to heat a greenhouse through the winter, so many places are in operation only from early spring through late fall. If one of these is in your area, inspect its merchandise, and if you find plants you want, watch for the end-of-the-season sale. If there's something you can't live without and only one is left at the time of the sale, buy it. But if you feel you can gamble on some items, wait until the last afternoon of the sale, gather together whatever you want, then make an offer on it. My rule of thumb is to offer half of what the sale price is. It's easier to come up in price than to go down. I've even been given free plants this way. The owners know that the plants will freeze, and they will have to haul them to the dump anyway, so they might as well give them away or sell them for next to nothing. Of course, there are exceptions. I found a huge pile of houseplants in a field behind a greenhouse. Surely, I thought, the owners would be more than happy to give them away. I was wrong. When I asked, the owner said they would be destroyed. I even asked if, perchance, he would consider donating them to a local nursing home. Again, the answer was no. His rationale was that if he gave any away, whoever got them would not need to buy any from him and he would lose money. In my opinion, what he failed to realize was that it would be good advertising. If a nurseryman gives me something for next-to-nothing (or free), I pass the word around that he is a good person to do business with. Of course, unless I know the person I'm talking with is a scrounger, I don't mention the super deal I got. If I can give someone a little free positive advertising, I will. Naturally, I tell the person to mention to the nursery owner that I sent him. This helps me out next time I go in to make a purchase.

THE OLD "HELP OUT WITH THE SALE" STRATEGY

You may recall that in the last chapter I told you to volunteer to help with gardening at a local park, historic site, or arboretum. If these places have plant sales and you volunteer to help set up and tear down, you have access to the best coming and going.

During setup, you get to see the cream of the crop. You can have first dibs before any of the general public is allowed to purchase. Of course, you have to pay for the items, but they'll probably be a lot less expensive than going to a nursery or greenhouse, and if you're a good worker, you might even get them at a discount (or free). Then at the end of the sale, you can clean up on the left-overs. And don't think there won't be anything good left. Sometimes the price on a plant is prohibitive, so people won't buy. When the sale is over, the people who did the pricing might finally figure out that this is why it didn't sell and substantially come down in price just to get rid of it.

Sometimes when people donate plants to such sales, they stipulate that they don't want them returned if they don't sell. It's easier for the folks who are holding the sale to get rid of the leftovers than to have to take care of them and hold them over until the next sale. At one sale at which I worked, the organizers were so glad to have the sale over that they didn't want to have anything left, so they gave away all the remaining plants. This is a hint to those of you who don't have the time or inclination to work at such a sale. Go late on the last day of the sale to get the "deals." Sometimes, too, everything is marked at half-price for the last part of the sale. If you see an advertisement for a sale and a phone number is listed, call and get the particulars. I usually try to get there for the opening to buy anything unusual or inexpensive, and then I go back as soon as I know the plants will be marked down.

Sometimes unlikely organizations have plant sales. The Audubon Society of which my cousin is a member had one. She mentioned it to me in passing, and I volunteered to help out. Am I a bird watcher? No. But I knew an extra hand could always be used, and anyone with some knowledge in the field would be especially useful. Not only did I get the before- and after-sale good-ies, but I got a tax deduction as a bonus. I donated a lot of my extra and disposable plants and used this donation as a write-off since the Audubon Society is a nonprofit organization.

THE OLD "BY-THE-WAY" TACTIC

Are you a rummage sale fanatic? Here's another prime source of plant material. You're right—I agree that you usually don't find a fine selection of landscape plants at a rummage sale. But does it hurt to drive by such a sale just to "case the joint"? Find a sale in a neighborhood where the landscaping is attractive, then stop by and see if you can find something you like. Take a glance at the rummage and then say, "Oh, by the way," and ask if you might buy a cutting, seeds, or whatever you happen to want. Even if the answer is no, it won't hurt to have asked. This works especially well at moving or estate sales, for obvious reasons. If the prices asked are outrageous, all you have to do is to say you're not interested at those prices. However, since you have taken a person by surprise, the general tendency is for a lower price to be quoted than if he or she had more of a chance to think about it. Naturally, if you want one of a pair of matched mugho pines that are flanking an entry, I think you should forget it. You have to use some discretion.

If you like rummage sales, you probably go to flea markets too. Especially in the spring and fall, when people are cleaning up their gardens and dividing plants, you'll find quite a number of plants sold at flea markets. Occasionally, people have an inflated sense of value, and prices will be out of line. Perhaps someone may even have sentimental attachments to a plant since the original came from Aunt Martha or some other relative or friend. But usually prices are very reasonable. For instance, once I found a table of many varieties of dwarf iris at a flea market. The woman had bought them several years ago, she told me, paid retail price, planted them, and found that they multiplied so fast in her small yard that they were literally taking over. She had given them to her neighbors and friends until they didn't want any more, and finally she decided to try the flea market. I bought these at less than wholesale price, and they were nicely potted, in bloom, and tagged with their individual names. Of course, since I bought a dozen, she made a special deal with me. In about three more years however, I'm afraid I'm going to have to try a booth at the flea market to sell the extras. Since I bought them so reasonably, I'll be able to sell them for even less than she did. Hopefully, I will make a bundle of money and will find more plants to buy. And the cycle goes on.

Another tactic that works well at flea markets is to take along in your car a few plants that you are using for trading stock. Instead of purchasing plants outright, ask the sellers if they would be willing to trade for what you have in the car. Often they aren't, but it's worth a try. I've found that people who are just starting a small nursery operation often try to supplement their incomes by taking some of their stock to a flea market. In this case, if your trading stock is unusual, there's a good chance that they will be interested. They will probably use your plants as "mother plants" and propagate more for sale.

Again, engage the people who are selling plants in conversation. Even if you don't want what they have to offer, stop to talk anyway. You never know what they have at home that they haven't brought along. You might even be able to inveigle an invitation to their garden, and who knows what you might find there.

THE OLD "BE SOMEONE YOU'RE NOT" PLAN

Have a lot of courage? Try this one. Most areas have a regional landscaping, gardening, or floral convention. If you can put on a good act, you can come away with some super deals even though these conventions generally are not open to the public. But how do you find out where and when they're being held? That's the tough part. I found out about my first one by being in the right place at the right time. I was at a nursery checking out an end-of-the-season sale when I happened to glance into a wastebasket sitting by the checkout counter. And what did I see? Sitting right on the top was a postcard that advertised a landscape conference only about fifty miles away. I surreptitiously copied the return address and wrote for information. Since I had no letterhead that made me sound like a landscaper, I typed a postcard and used my last name followed by "and Associates." I did not say I was in the business; I just requested information. I figured the request was a good gamble. It paid off. I got the information, a preregistration form, and even a schedule of seminars. What I was most interested in was the last day of the show. I needed to know when it would close. I did not preregister—I simply arrived the afternoon of the last day. By that time, regulations had been relaxed and registration was a breeze. With my information packet in hand when I approached the desk, I did not look like someone who had just wandered in off the street. I paid my four dollars to get in (I had brought my husband along for moral support), and the only questions we were asked was what field we were in (for example, retail, wholesale, nursery, landscape, etc.). Since I *was* landscaping the yard, I decided it wouldn't be too much of a fib to say I was a landscaper. They put that on our name tags and in we went. It was heaven. There was an enormous room filled with booths of everything from tools and chemicals to plants. I took a quick look around at everything just to see what was available and then went through again, deciding on what I really was interested in. Since it was the end of the show, many salespeople were selling the display items they had brought so they wouldn't have to pack them up and take them back. Then, of course, many were giving out free samples. I got enough samples of different kinds of fertilizers to take care of my yard for a year. One company was even kind enough to provide large shopping bags for all the promotional items that were given out. We came home with five bags of goodies. My husband and I each took a sample of anything we could find. That in itself was worth the drive and the four-dollar entry fee, but as we were walking around we also picked up *wholesale* catalogs and signed up on mailing lists. Often wholesalers' requirements are prohibitive—for example, before they will sell to you, you might have to provide three references of people in the trade with whom you've done business; or you may be required to order a minimum of $1,000 worth of plants; or you must agree to order in lots of twenty-five of one variety. However, many small local companies don't have these restrictions, and after perusing all the catalogs I picked up I found several from which I ordered. When you send in an order (with a money order, of course—a personal check doesn't do the trick) and the money is staring them in the face, it's difficult for them to send it back. Maybe the person who receives my orders is in a good mood when he sees the money order. I don't know. All I know is that it has worked for me.

When the salespeople were taking down their displays, I went back to see the plants in which I was particularly interested and asked what kind of close-out deals were being made. Some of the salespeople wouldn't come down from the prices they had been quoting all day (which were wholesale to start with); others weren't selling anything since their items had to be ordered. But others were tickled to get rid of things they wouldn't have to pack and take back. I made several deals that way, but the one I'm most proud of made me the owner of thirty-five dwarf rhododendrons. I paid less than thirty cents each for them. What in heaven's name did I do with all those rhodies, you ask? I kept one of each variety for myself, gave some for Christmas presents, and sold the rest at slightly over my cost to friends and neighbors. At that price, anyone who knew anything about the price of dwarf rhododendrons was very pleased to get them.

At a different booth, I acquired three free rose bushes (named varieties, no less). I had been admiring one bush every time I walked past it, but I didn't want it badly enough to pay even the wholesale price. A woman in the booth wouldn't budge when I tried to get her to reduce her price. Unfortunately, my husband was off examining rototillers somewhere (no, he didn't get us a free one—there *is* a limit to what we can get for nothing), so I couldn't "bring in the reserves." He has better luck dealing with women; I work better with men. Anyway, it wasn't that big a deal, so I went on. At the very end of the day, when the displays were being dismantled, we were walking down the aisle when I saw a man who looked like Grumpy of the Seven Dwarfs pushing a cartful of plants. There was the rose bush I liked. Since we were going in the same direction, we walked along with the cart and I pointed the rose out to my husband. The man overheard and asked if I liked it. Naturally, I gave him my biggest smile and wistfully said yes. With the sour expression he had on his face, I figured there would be no deal. But to my surprise, he said, "If you like it, take it." I grabbed. Then to top it off, he said, "There's two more different kinds in there. Want them?" What a silly question! I now have lovely 'Arizona,' 'Charisma,' and 'Gene Boerner' rose bushes in my yard.

My last acquisition for the day was potting soil. My husband, being the gentleman that he is (although I knew his ulterior motive), helped a woman who was struggling to get a dozen large boxes loaded onto a dolly. As a gesture of appreciation, she gave us another box from her display. It contained twenty-eight individually packaged two-quart bags of sterile potting soil.

When you're scouting these places, remember that sales representatives of large companies run some of the booths. They are the easiest to hit up for freebies. Most of them have a stock of items that are used for advertising purposes and that have to be given away in a certain amount of time. It's no money out of anyone's pocket, and you're actually doing the sales representatives a favor by taking the free items. When the representative is from a smaller firm, it's a different story. Then I back off the freebies and just try to make good deals since small companies don't have the advertising and promotional budget that large ones do.

Once I've registered for one of the conferences, I'll be sent information on others. If you aren't as lucky as I was and haven't found a notice lying around someplace, perhaps you could try the local library. If it happens to subscribe to a wholesale landscape or nursery magazine, you'll find conventions and conferences advertised there. Try the county agent too. He might be aware of such shows. If you have no luck, call the nearest convention center and ask if a show is scheduled. Shows usually are planned quite a bit in advance, so you should be able to find out about any within the next year. Also get the name of the person in charge and write for information. If that doesn't work, befriend the wife of a nursery owner and pick her brain.

If you don't have quite enough intestinal fortitude to crash a wholesale show, try the same tactics at a retail show. Home and garden or landscaping shows abound in every city of any size. A friend of mine went to a retail Christmas show, stuck around after closing, and picked some nice goodies out of waste baskets. It's absolutely amazing what people will throw away when they're tired.

THE OLD AUCTION GAME

"Auctions!" you say, clutching your throat and rolling your eyes. People seldom consider an auction a good source of plants. Lots of people panic at the mere mention of the word. It brings to their minds visions of Aunt Sally scratching her nose and buying a life-size stuffed hippopotamus or of your sister who thought she was buying one set of sheets for four dollars and later found out that she had purchased twenty sets at four dollars each. Fear no more. Here are some rules to follow that I guarantee will keep you out of trouble and will get you some mighty good buys too.

Rule 1: Get to the auction early and inspect the merchandise. Do not, I repeat, do not bid on anything that you have not seen close up no matter how good it looks from a distance. Creatures such as spider mites and mealybugs cannot be seen from across the room, and even though this doesn't mean that you shouldn't bid on the plant if it has some insects, the problem must be taken into account when you make your bid. (I'll discuss more about these and other pests in Chapter 6, "The Infirmary." Most auctioneers sell items "as is, where is," which means "what you sees is what you gets." So be sure to see it and see it up close before you get it—or get stuck with it, whichever the case may be.

Rule 2: As you look over the merchandise, jot down a list of those items that appeal to you and put the maximum price you are willing to pay next to each item. It is important to set prices while you're cool and calm. Do not go over that price. People will bid higher than they normally would for an item because they get carried away in the excitement of the auction and don't know when to stop. When you write down your top price, all you have to do is look at the list in your hand and you'll *know* when to stop no matter how excited you are. And always write down an uneven number. Use twelve dollars and fifty cents rather than ten dollars as your top price. Most other people who write down their top bids will stop at an even number, so if you go one bid higher, you'll get what you want and for little more.

How do you know a good deal? Generally, merchandise is somewhat itemized in auction advertisements. For instance, the advertisement might mention ten red maple trees in five-gallon containers. If there is no itemization, call the auctioneer or owner and ask him to list what will be for sale. Write down those plants you are interested in as he lists them for you. Then either go to a nursery and get prices on comparable plants, or if you're as lazy as I am and like to save gas and time, call. You can pretend you're interested in purchasing these items and ask their cost. This is the retail price. Depending on how unusual the item is and how badly I want it, I generally don't go over half of retail price on my bids at the auction. Also remember to take the plant's condition into account.

Rule 3: It is best to sit or stand up front so the auctioneer can see you. Auctioneers have a tendency to take a bid from someone up close rather than in the rear of the audience. Get the auctioneer's attention for your first bid by raising your hand. Don't be afraid to hold your hand high. The hardest bid to see and therefore the one most often missed is a hand held barely belt high. Once an auctioneer has you pegged as an active bidder for that item, he well continue to watch you, so you won't have to be concerned about his missing your bid as you might have had you waited to get his attention toward the end of the bidding.

Rule 4: Don't always wait for the lowest possible starting bid. If the auctioneer starts an item out by asking five dollars for a plant and you know that getting it for two dollars would be a steal, don't hope he'll drop all the way to fifty cents so you can start bidding there. Everyone will know it's a steal then, and even if they're not particularly interested in it, they'll start bidding and you've lost your chance. This will invite competitors to join in who might never have bid at all. If you had raised your hand when the auctioneer asked for two dollars, others might not have bid to begin with. Chances are, they're interested in it if it's practically free, but not otherwise.

Rule 5: Don't be afraid to ask questions. If you are not a regular auction-goer, there will often be quite a number of things you don't understand. Would you rather look "kinda dumb" to a bunch of people you'll probably never see again, or go home with a flat of cactus when you live in a swamp? If you're not sure which plant is being bid on, whether the auctioneer is asking for fifteen or fifty dollars, or whether you're bidding on one plant with the option of taking more or are required to take the whole flat, ask.

If you don't know how to indicate that you want to offer only half of the raise the auctioneer is looking for, ask the auctioneer or one of his assistants before the sale begins. For example, if ten dollars has been bid on a plant and the auctioneer is asking for fifteen, would you know how to let him know you wanted to bid twelve dollars and fifty cents? If not, ask. It can save you some money. And as my mother always says, "A penny is a penny."

Rule 6: Look for good deals at the beginning and end of the auction. At the start, people aren't psyched up yet and are hesitant to bid, so you may be able to get some steals. At the end, some folks have spent all the money they want to, others have no more space in their vehicles for more plants, many have left, and most are too tired to get excited about bidding anyway. At any rate, the auctioneer isn't going to beg and cajole buyers to up bids. This is the time to become active, and you'll get some fantastic buys, if, of course, they are items you want.

Rule 7: Have a readily accessible way to get your purchases home and have some place to put them when you get there. Once you buy something, it is your responsibility, even if you haven't paid for it yet. Or if the auctioneer says you can pick up items the next day, if left overnight, they will usually not be watered or cared for in any way. If someone accidentally tips one over while getting his plants, it will probably stay that way. Sometimes your plants may even grow legs and walk away if left unattended. When I go to a plant auction, I usually accumulate about twice what I think I'll get, so I always plan my transportation accordingly. At one sale I attended, the prices were so low I even found it economical to rent a self-drive truck to cart them away.

Now that you know what to do and what not to do at auctions, where do you find them? Most newspapers have a special column in the classified section where nursery overstock auctions and going-out-of-business auctions are listed. You might also find them listed under special categories, such as columns marked "For Sale: Nursery Stock." After a month or two of watching the classified ads, you'll know exactly where auctions are listed. Or, if you're impatient, call the newspaper and ask under which category nursery auctions are generally listed.

An auction is one of the exceptions to the rule of not driving too far to get plant material. I have driven more than fifty miles to a nursery auction because I knew the reasonable prices and amount I could purchase would make it worthwhile. Be sure that you have a whole day to spend, however, because auctions of this type usually take at least that long. This is the place to stock up on larger items, plants that your friends and neighbors aren't likely to want to part with, or ones that take too long to grow from seeds or cuttings, such as large shrubs and trees. Of course, if you're like me, you'll buy anything that is a steal if you like it. I figure out afterwards where to put it. Or I use it for trading stock.

I went to a local greenhouse auction and was amazed at a woman who seemed to be interested in buying something only one other person was half-heartedly bidding on. At this sale, the customers were lucky because the auctioneer did not know a marigold from a petunia and the owner was not present to identify the items people were bidding on. Therefore, the people who knew about plants got what they wanted at good prices, and those who didn't bought plants and didn't even know what they were. The woman I mentioned was buying pots with nothing but soil and weeds in them. Everyone thought she was a bit strange, and being curious I examined one of the pots. As I looked closely, I could see the yellow and brown remains of what looked like large blades of grass. It finally dawned on me that those pots were full of bulbs that had already bloomed, died back, and were in their resting stage. I felt she deserved to have a corner on the market since she was smart enough to figure this out from the start, so I refrained from bidding against her. Luckily for me, she soon had enough bulbs and stopped bidding. This is when I stepped in, bid, and got some magnificent buys. Had I started bidding against her, we both would have had to pay much higher prices. I guess I was just lucky she wasn't a dealer who wanted them all. That was a chance I had to take. In the group of bulbs I brought home that day, I not only got hardy bulbs like tulip and daffodil, but also got fifteen pots of top-size amaryllis bulbs for less than fifty cents each. Check the price of amaryllis bulbs and see what kind of a deal that was. Of course, if the woman had purchased all the bulbs, I still had the option to talk to her later, offer her more than what she paid for the ones I wanted, and ask if she would sell.

Sometimes you can even make a deal before the auction begins. Often, in the interest of time, an auctioneer will sell half a dozen or more of the same thing to one bidder. But many people, for example, don't want six 'Nelly Moser' clematis. If you see someone acting very interested in an item you want, don't hesitate to approach this person. Outline your plan of joining forces to bid on this plant, and see if you can strike a deal. Be sure to decide which of you will do the bidding and what your top price will be; otherwise, if you happen to be across the room when the item comes up, you might find yourself bidding against your partner. Also decide ahead of time how many each of you wants. Naturally, when it comes time to auction those plants, there is a chance that they will be sold one at a time, but it isn't likely. Unless it's a small sale, there is usually so much merchandise that the auctioneer is forced to sell more than one plant at a time. If an auction takes too long, the auctioneer will lose bidders, and with fewer bidders, the prices can go down.

Not all of the plant auctions I go to are run by large nurseries or are all-day affairs. I've made some excellent buys at small auctions. One in particular was the local Rhododendron Society auction. I saw it mentioned in the gardening section of the newspaper and decided to give it a try. All the rhodies were donated by members, so I knew it would not be a large auction. The first several plants went for such high prices that I was ready to walk out. Then I realized that the reason for the high bids was that those plants were the more unusual varieties. When the common ones came up for bid, there was little interest by the crowd because most bidders were rhodie enthusiasts who had all the usual varieties and were more interested in the uncommon kinds. I was interested in anything inexpensive, so I got what the collectors didn't want at darn good prices and was pleased with my purchases.

5

Walk (Don't Tromp) on the Wild Side

Before becoming citified, my husband and I lived in the country. When transactions to purchase a house in town were in their final stages, we knew that we would move into our new home within the month. We began, therefore, to eye the landscaping (or lack of) of our new home more seriously. This became one of the prominent points of conversation during our walks in the countryside. We were lucky to live across the road from a small creek that ran through cultivated fields, and we often took walks along that little waterway. Here we found a multitude of ferns growing, and since I had always loved ferns I decided to dig a few to take with us. We had a little alcove on the north side of our new house that seemed to be the ideal spot for them since here it would always be shady and very moist. This is something that creates many problems for people who try to transplant wild plants. Most people fail to realize that a shade-loving plant that grows in very rich, well-drained soil will not (repeat, *will not*) take kindly to being transplanted to clay soil on the south side of a home. It will almost certainly die, and I don't blame it.

Whenever a plant is taken from its previous surroundings (particularly from the wild), it must be provided with similar conditions. If it has been living with its feet in water, chances are it will need those conditions again to stay healthy. Oh, it may survive, but it won't look healthy or perhaps won't even bloom.

One factor that the novice often fails to take into consideration is that if a woodland plant had been growing in the sunlight in early spring and then is put in a sunny spot in the garden, it probably won't survive. Many such plants like to have plenty of sunlight early in the season, but after they have bloomed they need shade. During the flowering period, there are no leaves on the trees to shade them, but by the time they are through, the tree leaves have come out and filter the sun considerably. Keep this in mind on your jaunts through the woods. Some of the plants that would fit into this category are: jack-in-the-pulpit (*Arisaema triphyllum*), Solomon's seal (*Polygonatum* various), trailing arbutus (*Epigaea repens*), trillium (*Trillium* various), and violet (*Viola* various).

THE PILLAGE PROBLEM

By all means don't go wandering through the countryside digging up people's front yards even though they do look woodsy. A friend who lives in the country may be a good source of plant material. Or, if you're driving down a country road and spot some nice wildflowers in an area that is being grazed, you can pretty well be certain that the owners are not trying to conserve a bit of the environment. If you were to go to the house and ask permission to dig a few, you'd probably get an okay. Even if you dig up plants from along the roadside right-of-way, don't totally denude the area of that particular type of plant. Not only for conservation, but for aesthetics as well, take one here and one there. Just don't indiscriminately dig up a whole area, and don't take any plants from a park or protected area.

As I mentioned in a previous chapter, it's a good idea to get to know some real estate people. They can let you know when a natural area is slated to undergo development—for example, when a subdivision or factory is going to be built on the site. In cases like these, I feel that it is perfectly all right to go in (with permission, of course) and dig wildflowers even if they are on the protected list. Developers usually start by bulldozing the area anyway, so if that's the case, I feel I'm doing my bit toward conservation by rescuing the plants. I have even dug plants in situations like these when I didn't want or need them, just to save them. Then I gave them to friends or donated them to a park or historic site. Just be sure to explain what special care and conditions they will need.

I have occasionally tried to move trees from soon-to-be-developed areas. For me, it just plain doesn't work. Usually they are competing with other trees and have one side that's beautiful and other sides that often leave a lot to be desired. Another problem is that they don't transplant as easily as wildflowers since you need to take a lot more of the root ball (soil around the roots) with the tree. If you are observant, you can possibly find a small symmetrical seedling that will transplant more easily. Just take a large root ball and a bucket of the soil that it has been growing in so planting it in its new home won't be such a shock to the roots. Remember, however, that a seedling tree will take quite a few years to reach any size, so be prepared to be patient with it.

Late fall or early spring is the best time to transplant. If those times are impossible, it is usually best to wait until after a plant has finished blooming. If this is the case, it's a good idea to mark the plant with a stick pushed into the ground. I've lost many plants by failing to do this. In the early spring, it is easy to see all the plants, particularly when they're flowering. But wait for a month until the grass grows up and there are no flowers to go back to, or until the plants have died back entirely; you'll swear that you're in an entirely different place. So mark what you want, just in case.

MULCH YOUR WAY TO A SLIMMER, TRIMMER YOU

Once your wild plants have been transplanted, it's a good idea to mulch them. If they have come out of a wooded area, they will be accustomed to having layers of leaves and other plant debris over their roots. You can duplicate this by using leaf mold gathered from the plant's original home or by using rotten manure, sawdust, wood chips, pine needles, newspaper, or straw (not hay).

This is how my husband learned the difference between hay and straw. Being a city boy, he was late to learn about many outside-type things. When we moved to our new house, I knew I would need a lot of mulch, but since I was reluctant to buy bark chips or other such expensive stuff, I sent him out to the country to get a pick-up load of straw. He came back within a short time, announcing that the mission had been accomplished and that he had unloaded the bales on the patio. The next day, I had a lot on my mind and did not pay much attention to the "straw" until I had already put a half a bale on one of the beds. It was then that I realized my husband's mistake. He had brought home hay instead of straw! The difference is, basically, that hay is the whole plant, seeds and all; straw is just the plant's stem. In other words, as I was mulching with the hay, I was also spreading the seeds from it. Needless to say, my husband got a quick lesson in what's what and I spent quite a bit of time weeding the greenery that grew up in the mulched area.

Mulching performs two main functions for your wild plants. It helps smother weeds that may try to germinate, and it also helps to retain moisture. You still have to weed, though; it's just easier. By retaining moisture, mulch makes it unnecessary to water as often; it saves time and helps cut down on water bills if free water is not available.

I took a class in landscaping when we moved to the Pacific Northwest because many landscape plants common to this area were unfamiliar to me and I wanted to give them proper treatment. One of the points made by my instructor was the importance of soil improvement. He advocated putting three inches of rotted manure on each bed twice a year, once in late fall and again in early spring. If you follow this procedure for six years, he said, no matter what your soil was like to start with, it would be perfect by the end of that time. The manure does not even need to be worked in; the worms do that part of the job for you. The thought of hauling all that manure did not really excite me, but as many areas of my yard were heavy clay, I knew that I would have to do something. The section I had decided would be my wildflower garden was especially bad. Woodland flowers, in particular, need to have a well-drained, humus-type soil. They would not fare well in clay. I called various stables in the area to inquire about manure and finally settled on one that seemed best to me. The horses were not pastured where they could graze on any weeds and the bedding used was sawdust rather than straw. This combination would cut down on the weeds I would bring in with the manure and also would make it easier to handle. I find that straw tends to mat and is therefore more difficult to spread. My husband, being almost as tight as I am, brought up the cost of gas for this project. The place I had chosen to get the manure was about a twenty-minute drive from our house, and even though it was free, the gas wasn't. I calculated it would take about twenty pick-up loads to cover our beds with the right amount of manure. My husband figured the cost of gas to make twenty trips and it was by no means inexpensive. I thought of the aching muscles I would acquire and almost decided not to bother. Then my pennypinching spirit got the better of me and I figured out a way to rationalize the project. I was a tad bit overweight and was planning to take an exercise class. Since there was a class fee involved and I would have to drive to and from the class, I rationalized that I could forget the class and get my exercise hauling manure, thus coming out about equal on cost.

THE "CLASSY" SIDE

About the time I was hauling manure, I received a brochure that advertised a one-night class on wildflowers. I am on the mailing list of several organizations that offer free or inexpensive classes to the public, and I was most interested in this latest one. Unfortunately, I had a previous commitment on the night it was offered and so I was unable to attend. I did manage to convince my husband to go, however, and this proved to be a happy alternative. The people who taught the seminar not only lectured and showed beautiful color slides that helped to spark my husband's interest, but they also offered a selection of free wildflower seeds. This is actually how I got interested in growing wildflowers from seed. Now, not only is my husband a wildflower enthusiast, but as a bonus I got free seeds and know who to call if I can't identify a wild plant or if I have trouble getting it to grow.

Call around to see if there are such classes offered in your area. The ones I take are often one-night classes and cover a diverse selection of subjects. I've taken everything from a mini-course on mushroom identification to wildflower propagation. These classes have always been very worthwhile. Even if I don't get free samples, I get worlds of knowledge and I usually meet interesting and informative people. (Play your cards right and you can get free samples from them, whether they're your instructors or classmates.)

KID POWER

I have no children, but a friend of mine told me an interesting method of acquiring wildflowers by using "kid power." Whenever they take a trip or vacation, the children take along paper bags and collect various wildflower seeds. They write information on the bag on where and when the seed was collected, what the plant looked like, and what its habitat was. If they know the name of it, that's included too, of course. If not, they make a trip to the local library when they return to identify their "unknowns." This friend says her three children have really become interested in these seed-hunting expeditions. They've learned how to tell if a seed is ripe, how to identify certain plant families, and are now learning about edible wild plants. Of course, the children are responsible for growing their own seeds, and each has a coffee can in the refrigerator to keep their finds until they're ready to plant. Many seeds need to be stratified (given a cold period) before they will germinate. A stint in the refrigerator or freezer fools them into thinking they have gone through a winter season, and they will sprout. Be certain the seeds are completely dry before refrigerating them or you may have a problem with mold. Each of my friend's children has his own bit of the yard for his wildflower garden and is quite proud of it.

What looks especially nice to me in a yard is to have a small area devoted to wildflowers. You can naturalize bulbs into the grassy areas and have random clusters of other wild plants scattered about. I say scattered because in my opinion one of the least attractive things done with wild plants is to put them in nice orderly rows or to place them symmetrically. That's not how they grow in the wild, and it seems unnatural. I like to see them as they were growing in their original homes. Of course, this is just my personal preference.

WOODLAND, ETC.

Many plants can be transplanted and do very well in a landscaped environment. Most ferns, as I previously mentioned, are fairly adaptable. Any of the many species look especially nice when combined with violet (*Viola* various), Solomon's seal (*Polygonatum* various), or mayapple (*Podophyllum peltatum*). If you don't know what these look like, get a book from the local library with pictures of wildflowers.

Again, I remind you to leave some for the next person to enjoy and don't dig any plants (or even pick the flowers, for that matter) that are on the protected list. Call your county extension agent if you're not sure what's protected. If you have your heart set on one that is protected, break down, spend a little money, and buy it through a nursery. You can find quite a number that carry a good selection of wildflowers listed in gardening periodicals. Again, try the wholesale route.

I've been discussing primarily woodland wildflowers because they're my favorite, are readily available where I live, and fit best into my landscape plans. The same general rules also apply to other types of wild plants—from desert to prairie to alpine. Recreate the proper environment, and you'll have little trouble growing them.

Desert plants have been particularly hard hit by people who have dug them indiscriminately for their landscapes. I have even been told about people who have gone into the business of "plantnapping." It seems some of the large old saguaro, (*Carnegiea gigantea*) and barrel cactus (*Ferocactus* various) can bring quite a bit of money on the black market. And some people are always ready to make a fast buck. Please check with the county agent before adding any cactus (or any other wild plant) to your landscape. Many companies now sell packets of seeds labeled "woodland" or "desert" or "prairie." They contain a variety of species and the directions to grow them. I'd rather spend a dollar on a packet of seeds than risk disturbing an environment. There's a limit to pennypinching.

In the following tables (Tables 5-1, 5-2, 5-3, 5-4, and 5-5), I have tried to give you an idea of which wildflowers will do well in specific environments. There are thousands of species that I haven't listed. Just because I haven't mentioned a particular plant that does not necessarily mean that it doesn't adapt well to being domesticated. It just means that there is not room to list all the possible choices.

For example, bellflower (*Campanula* various) has a species that will grow in almost any environment in the United States. The fact that I have one listed for the mountainous areas does not indicate that there is not another species that will grow in a woodland environment. Many species will adapt to several environments and do equally well in all of them.

Some seeds will take several years to germinate or will take many years to bloom after they sprout. If so, I did not list "seed" as a method of propagation, even though they may be propagated this way. Often there are several methods that can be used; I simply tried to choose the easiest.

To find directions on how to propagate plants by these methods, read Chapter 7, "The Maternity Ward."

Some plants are commonly found in many nurseries; others are found only in those nurseries that specialize in wildflowers. If, in the tables, I have indicated that a plant can be found in a nursery, this means it is fairly easy to find in many. A plant not marked like this does not mean it will never be found in a nursery, it just means it's not as likely to be found there.

One final word about the tables. When I say a plant is easy to grow, I mean it's easy only if it's put into the proper environment and cared for correctly. Canada anenome (*Anenome canadensis*) is extremely easy to grow in a woodland environment, but take it to a desert situation and its chances are slim. Or plant it in a woodland environment in midsummer, don't water it, and I'll be willing to bet that you won't see it come spring. Just let common sense be your guide with wildflowers, and I'm sure you'll have a good measure of success.

TABLE 5-1

Woodland Wildflowers

NAME	TYPE AND PROPAGATION METHOD	COMMENTS
American bugbane (*Circumfuga americana*)	Perennial; seedling	Late summer bloom
American twinleaf (*Jeffersonia diphylla*)	Perennial; division	Produces interesting seed pods
Bloodroot (*Sanguinaria canadensis*)	Perennial; division	Often found in nurseries
Blue cohosh (*Caulophyllum thalictroides*)	Perennial; division	Easy to grow
Canada anenome (*Anenome canadensis*)	Perennial; root division	Easy to grow
Dog-tooth violet (*Erythronium* various)	Perennial; corm	Lily-like flowers
Dutchman's-breeches (*Dicentra cucullaria*)	Perennial; division	Often found in nurseries
False Solomon's seal (*Smilacina racemosa*)	Perennial; rhizome division	Fragrant flowers
Hairy fairy-bells (*Disporum lanuginosum*)	Perennial; seed	Red berries
Mayapple (*Podophyllum peltatum*)	Perennial; seed	Produces yellow "apples"
Partridgeberry (*Mitchella repens*)	Evergreen; stem cuttings	Good fragrant ground cover
Round-lobed liverleaf (*Hepatica americana*)	Perennial; seed	Self-seeds
Solomon's seal (*Polygonatum biflorum*)	Perennial; seed	Self-seeds
Trailing arbutus (*Epigaea repens*)	Shrub; stem layering	Fragrant flowers
White baneberry (*Actaea pachypoda*)	Perennial; seed	Very easy to grow; berries poisonous
White wake-robin (*Trillium grandiflorum*)	Perennial; rhizome division	Often found in nurseries
Wild ginger (*Asarum canadense*)	Perennial; root division	Very easy to grow

TABLE 5-2

Desert Wildflowers

NAME	TYPE AND PROPAGATION METHOD	COMMENTS
Adam's-needle yucca (*Yucca filamentosa*)	Perennial; root division	Fire-retardant
Beardlip penstemon (*Penstemon barbatus*)	Perennial; seed	Attracts hummingbirds; self-seeds
Blazing-star (*Mentzelia laevicaulis*)	Perennial; seed	Flowers open in evening; self-seeds
California rock cress (*Arabis blepharophylla*)	Perennial; root division	Very pest-resistant
Century plant (*Agave americana*)	Perennial; off-shoots	Fire-retardant
Desert marigold (*Baileya multiradiata*)	Annual; seed	Self-seeds
Desert mariposa (*Calochortus Kennedyi*)	Perennial; corm	Grass-like leaves
Gum plant (*Grindelia robusta*)	Perennial; seed	Grows to four feet tall
Live forever (*Dudleya saxosa*)	Shrub; leaf cutting	Succulent; very drought-resistant
Matilija poppy (*Romneya coulteri*)	Perennial; off-shoots	Very fragrant
Mexican tulip poppy (*Hunnemannia fumariaefolia*)	Perennial; seed	Self-seeds
Moth mullein (*Verbascum blattaria*)	Biennial; seed	Self-seeds
Prickly poppy (*Argemone hispida*)	Annual; seed	Very easy to grow
Sand verbena (*Abronia umbellata*)	Perennial; seed	Good for erosion control; fragrant
Sego lily (*Calochortus nuttallii*)	Perennial; corm	Early summer bloom
Teddy-bear cactus (*Opuntia bigelovii*)	Perennial; seed or pads	Grows to eight feet tall
Wild hyacinth (*Triteleia hyacinthina*)	Perennial; corm	Dislikes water in summer

TABLE 5-3

Mountain Wildflowers

NAME	TYPE AND PROPAGATION METHOD	COMMENTS
Baby blue-eyes (Nemophila menziesii)	Annual; seed	Very easy to grow
Bear grass (Xerophyllum tenax)	Perennial; seed	Large grass used as accent
Bitter root (Lewisia rediviva)	Perennial; seed	Often found in nurseries
California fuchsia (Zauschneria californica)	Perennial; division	Attracts birds
Checkerberry wintergreen (Gaultheria procumbens)	Evergreen; rhizome division	Good ground cover; attracts birds
Chinese houses (Collinsia heterophylla)	Annual; seed	Good for cut flowers
Corn lily (Clintonia borealis)	Perennial; rhizome division	Slightly difficult to transplant
Fireweed (Epilobium angustifolium)	Perennial; seed	Very easy to grow
Fleabane (Erigeron peregrinus)	Perennial; seed	Very easy to grow
Harebell (Campanula rotundifolia)	Perennial; root division	Often found in nurseries
Hooker evening primrose (Oenothera hookeri)	Biennial; seed	Often found in nurseries
Monkshood (Aconitum columbianum)	Perennial; seed	Needs constant Moisture
New England aster (Aster novae-angliae)	Perennial; root division	Grows to six feet tall
Owl's clover (Orthocarpus purpurascens)	Annual; seed	Self-seeds
Rock cress (Arabis blepharophylla)	Perennial; root division	Attractive year-round foliage
Spotted cranesbill (Geranium maculatum)	Perennial; rhizome division	Needs constant moisture
Wild indigo (Baptisia tinctoria)	Perennial; seed	Easy to grow

TABLE 5-4

Wetland Wildflowers

NAME	TYPE AND PROPAGATION METHOD	COMMENTS
Blue boneset (Eupatorium coelestinum)	Perennial; seed	Self-seeds
Blue flag (Iris versicolor)	Perennial; rhizome division	Roots are poisonous
Bunchberry (Cornus canadensis)	Perennial; offsets	Often found in nurseries
Cardinal flower (Lobelia cardinalis)	Perennial; root division	Often found in nurseries
Common camass (Camassia quamash)	Perennial; bulb	Bulb edible
Common goldthread (Coptis trifolia)	Perennial; rhizome division	Good ground cover
Cow parsnip (Heracleum sphondylium)	Perennial; seed	Very large plant
Douglas meadow foam (Limnanthes douglasii)	Annual; seed	Very easy to grow
Fringed gentian (Gentianopsis crinita)	Perennial; seed	A challenge to grow
Marsh marigold (Caltha palustris)	Perennial; seed	May be invasive
Meadow beauty (Rhexia virginica)	Perennial; tuber	Easy to grow
Rose mallow (Hibiscus moscheutos)	Perennial; stem cutting	Easy to grow
Rose mandarin (Streptopus roseus)	Perennial; rhizome division	Good ground cover
Swamp aster (Aster puniceus)	Perennial; root division	Easy to grow
Swamp milkweed (Asclepias incarnata)	Perennial; seed	Flowers attract butterflies
Turtlehead (Chelone lyonii)	Perennial; seed	Often found in nurseries
Virginia bluebells (Mertensia virginica)	Perennial; root division	Flowers attract bees

TABLE 5-5

Prairie Wildflowers

NAME	TYPE AND PROPAGATION METHOD	COMMENTS
Avens (Geum triflorum)	Perennial; root division	Often found in nurseries
Black-eyed susan (Rudbeckia hirta)	Biennial; seed	Very easy to transplant
Blanketflower (Gaillardia aristata)	Perennial; seed	Blooms first year from seed
Blue-eyed grass (Sisyrinchium angustifolium)	Perennial; root division	Grass-like leaves
California poppy (Eschscholtzia californica)	Perennial; seed	Self-seeds
Common shooting-star (Dodecatheon meadia)	Perennial; root division	Goes dormant in midsummer
Purple coneflower (Echinacea angustifolia)	Perennial; seed	Long bloom period
Red gilia (Ipomopsis rubra)	Annual; seed	Makes good cut flower
Satin flower (Clarkia amoena)	Annual; seed	Hard to transplant
Scarlet paintbrush (Castilleja coccinea)	Biennial; seed	Hard to transplant
Spiked gay-feather (Liatris spicata)	Perennial; root division	Seeds very slow to germinate
Star grass (Hypoxis hirsuta)	Perennial; corm	Seeds are hard to collect
Texas bluebonnet (Lupinus texensis)	Annual; seed	Hard to transplant; self-seeds
Tidy-tips (Layia platyglossa)	Annual; seed	Found in mixed wildflower seed packets
Unicorn root (Aletris farinosa)	Perennial; seed	Very easy to grow
Virginia strawberry (Fragaria virginiana)	Perennial; rooted runners	Edible ground cover
Wild bergamot (Monarda fistulosa)	Perennial; seed	Often found in nurseries

6

The Infirmary

Now you have an abundance of plants. But what do you do if your patio is full of pathetic little creatures rescued from alleys or rejected by nurseries? It is important to give them some loving care first, particularly if they were adopted in the heat of the summer. They're probably in shock and need time in a pot with a bit of water; pamper them with shade and a little pruning. If you put them immediately into the ground, especially if the temperatures are high, their root systems won't be able to send up the water as fast as they use it; they may even wilt and die. Above all, don't fertilize them, because fertilization at this time will cause a spurt of growth. Since the roots may not be in top-notch shape, they probably won't be able to keep up with the needs of the plant and they'll die. Usually if the plants have come from a nursery, they probably have been fertilized almost daily and can use a little rest. Keep in mind that I'm referring to plants that look sick or tired, not those that you purchased at a plant sale or some similar source where they had a healthy start.

CALL A SURGEON

If your plant is brown or wilted on the top, or some of the leaves are shrivelled, cut the stem back with a sharp knife to where there are healthy green leaves or a green stem. Always cut back to a node (that's a place on the stem, usually identified by a bump, where the leaves come out). If you don't, the stump that is left will probably rot and may injure the rest of the plant. At any rate, it will look ugly, and at this point in its life the poor plant needs all the beautification it can get.

There are no healthy leaves at all, you say? If it looks as though it may need massive surgery (everything above the soil line is shrivelled or all the leaves are brown and crispy), don't despair. Take the plant gently out of the pot, if it's in one, and check the roots. The best way to remove a plant from a pot is to put your hand over the top of the soil with the stem between your fingers. (I hope I needn't remind you to wear gloves when you work with roses or cactus.) Turn the pot over and lightly tap the bottom with the heel of your other hand. Most often this will be all the plant needs to make it come out. If this doesn't work, however, turn the pot up again and insert a butter knife around the edges, as if you're trying to get a cake out of a pan. Then go through the first steps again. If the pot is too big to do this, set it on its side and thump all the way around it with the heel of your hand. Then tug gently (very gently) on the lower part of the stem to release and slide the plant out. Once it is out, look at the color of the roots. If they are firm and whitish on the inside when you cut one in half, chances are that they will send up another shoot and survive. If they are brown all the way through and mushy, or brown and very brittle, chalk it up. If there are some roots that are brown all the way through and some that aren't, cut off the brown ones and proceed as if all the roots are good. If you have to cut off some of the roots, be sure to compensate by cutting off some of the top—that is, cut away half of the root and take off half the top of the plant. Again, cut just above a node. If the roots are in fairly good condition, they probably will make new top growth even if you had to cut the leaves and stem clear to the soil line. Just be patient with them. They'll take more time than others to recuperate.

If your plant has no leaves or stem after the "operation," be sure not to overwater it. A "roots only" plant does not need as much water as one with leaves on it since it does not need to send moisture to any top parts. If you have found brown squishy roots, this is almost a sure sign that the plant has been overwatered, and this overwatering is probably what caused the top parts to die. Hold back water altogether for a couple of days, or more rot might set in and damage the remaining good roots. A cactus, succulent, or anything with juicy stems or leaves can be left without water for several days to prevent rot spreading. A good idea in a case such as this is to cut back to healthy tissue, then dust the area with powdered charcoal. A good source of this is the fish tank-type charcoal. I use a rolling pin on it until it's very fine. Or whir it in your blender.

Late one summer I acquired a number of Rocky Mountain columbine, (*Aquilegia caerulea*) plants that had completely dry leaves and stems. Even the roots looked sad. But since I particularly wanted columbine and these were free, I decided to follow the advice I give to others and put them in my infirmary. I waited until fall with no results. Not even a hint of green peeked out of the soil. I took the plants out of the pots to throw them away (naturally, I was going to reuse the pots) and found that they had beautiful fat white roots. I knew that I couldn't keep them over the winter in their small pots, so even though they had no leaves, I put them into the ground. I ignored them all winter and the next spring had a wonderful display of columbine flowers. It became very clear to me that some plants can take a lot more abuse than others and still bounce back. After you've rescued some from the throes of death, you'll learn which species are survivors and which aren't.

Some plants are more difficult than most to transplant. Remember though that I said transplant, not plant. To me, the difference is that in transplanting you dig a plant out of the ground in one location and put it into the soil in another, while in planting you put a plant that has been grown in a pot into a prepared hole in the soil. It's easier to plant than to transplant.

Some plants that are harder to transplant than most are: Pacific dogwood (*Cornus nuttallii*), hollyhock (*Alcea rosea*), lupine (*Lupinus* various), magnolia (*Magnolia* various), maple (*Acer* various), oak (*Quercus* various), pecan (*Carya illinoinensis*), peony (*Paeonia* various), sassafras (*Sassafras albidum*), and shagbark hickory (*Carya ovata*).

As a general rule, plants with long tap roots such as a carrot has, or with fleshy roots, are the more difficult kinds to transplant.

CHOOSING THE HOSPITAL SITE

Now that all your "sickies" are potted, you'll probably notice that they're a tad bit on the homely side. So plan to locate your infirmary in an unobtrusive place. It should be situated in a shady area, either on the north side of a building or under a dense tree. If you live in a windy part of the country, you'll find they do better if they are protected from strong wind. Wind tends to dry both plants and soil and also can cause physical damage to the plant by whipping the stems or leaves if they are weak.

The time that a plant must be left potted in the infirmary will vary with the condition it's in and what kind of plant it is. Some that are in fair condition (or succulents and cactus, which can take more abuse) may take only a week to recover, while others may take a month or more. You'll know when to move them into your landscape when they stand up straighter, put on new growth, or look greener. When I ask someone the question "How do you know when . . . ?" I absolutely hate when they answer, "Oh, you'll just know." But that's my answer now. After you've taken a few basket cases and made them well, "you'll just know" when they've recovered. The plants will look better physically and you'll be able to see the difference. If you're not sure, knock them out of the pot and check the roots.

When the plants are well, the pots can be moved from total shade into partial sun. This is when it is important to know the best type of light situation for each plant. If they are shade lovers like most primroses (*Primula* various) or common bleeding hearts (*Dicentra spectabilis*), send them directly from the infirmary into the yard. If you have sun lovers like roses or many perennials, leave them in their pots and take them from the infirmary into partial sun for at least two weeks. In hotter climates or in the heat of the summer, it's best to leave them even longer. Then they can go into the ground in full sun. Failure to follow this procedure will probably cause shock, and they'll get sunburned and die. Even suntan lotion won't help them.

Once they've been transplanted into the yard, they will need to be watered more often than established plants in the hot part of the year. Most plants' roots will become adequately established in about a year, so the second hot season you can treat them just like your other plants.

THE BULB WARD

Bulbs are a slightly different story. Each bulb contains the tiny leaves, stem, and flowerbud to produce next year's plant. As long as the bulbs were not terribly overcrowded in previous years and are not diseased or rotted, they stand a good chance of flowering the year after you plant them. Keep in mind that the growing cycle of a bulb does not end until the leaves yellow and die. The foliage should be allowed to ripen naturally because it manufactures all the nutrients needed for the plant's future growth. So please do not tie the leaves in knots or make ponytails of them with rubber bands. This lessens the amount of leaf surface that is exposed to the sun and thereby reduces the bulb's food.

If the foliage is already growing and it's still green when you find the bulbs, they need to get more sun to finish "ripening." If you cut off the tops before the leaves turn yellow, next season's flower crop will be affected and you'll have fewer and/or smaller blooms. So if you have green leaves on your bulbs and they're in pots, leave them there, put the pots in a sunny spot, and water regularly until the tops begin to yellow. At this point, cut back on the water and allow the leaves to turn brown. The pots can then be stored in a dry place until planting time (usually fall), or if you're in a crunch for space, take the bulbs out of the pots and store them in onion bags, old nylons, or whatever you can think up that will let air circulate through the bulbs. Hang them up, if you can.

If the bulbs are loose when you find them, you can either plant them in pots or "heel them in." This means they should be placed in an unobtrusive spot in the garden and covered over with soil. It will be adequate to dig a trench and put the bulbs in with the tops sticking out of the soil. In this case, the bulbs can be lying on their sides; the foliage doesn't even need to be upright, just as long as it's not covered with soil. Then follow the directions as though the bulbs were in pots. If you get them with the foliage already brown, simply remove the foliage and store the bulbs, keeping them dry and cool.

If the bulbs you bring home still have flowers on them, remove the flowers. Then the bulbs will not have to expend energy on setting seed and will produce a better plant for next year. Keep this in mind with all the bulbs in your yard. As soon as the flowers fade, remove them. However, bulbs such as snowdrop (*Galanthus* various), squill (*Scilla* various), winter aconite (*Eranthis hyemalis*), cyclamen (*Cyclamen* various), glory-of-the-snow (*Chionodoxa* various), and grape hyacinth (*Muscari* various) may self-seed, so remove the flowers only if you don't want them to multiply themselves this way.

When you plant the bulbs in the fall, follow this general rule: If a bulb is greater than two inches in diameter, plant it at a depth of three times the diameter. If it is less than two inches, plant it at a depth of four times its diameter. If the soil has good drainage, it should go about one or two inches deeper because many bulbs will last longer when planted more deeply and also will produce larger flowers.

Don't forget to add bonemeal to the soil. The poor bulbs have probably been neglected or have suffered from being overcrowded. They can use the boost bonemeal gives. It's not an instant shot-in-the-arm that produces results immediately; it's more like a time-release substance. So have patience. The flowers that are produced the first flowering season after planting are a product of the conditions surrounding the bulb the previous year. So even if you do everything right, the flower production may be very skimpy. But if you've given the bulbs bonemeal and some space to grow, they'll most likely produce a lot more flowers and larger ones the second year.

In warm winter areas it is necessary to give bulbs such as daffodil and tulip an artificial winter by refrigerating them for six to eight weeks before planting. Then, after they have been planted, have bloomed and the foliage has died back, they must be dug again and stored until it's time for the refrigeration process again. If the bulbs are left in the ground, they won't bloom the next year. They need cold to bloom. If you live in such an area, check with a reputable nursery owner to see which types of bulbs need this treatment.

Some sections of the country have a problem with narcissus bulb flies that lay eggs on the foliage and whose larvae eat holes in the bulbs. Find out from your county agent if the fly is a problem in your area and what steps are recommended for protection.

GOT BUGS?

If the invalid plants have come as cast-offs from a nursery, they may have been discarded because they suffered from insects or disease. Although problems like these can be picked up anywhere, they often occur on plants that have been sitting around a nursery for too long. Most likely, they've just become potbound and weakened, and have contracted a problem. It's just like you. When you're under stress or are physically weak, you're more apt to pick up a "bug."

A spider mite infestation makes the plant look as if it's dusty. Look closely, and if you see tiny webs that resemble those of a spider between the stem and leaf or on the undersurface of the leaf, this means a severe case (see Figure 6-1). Spider mites suck out the plants' juices and weaken them. The most economical way to get rid of mites is to take a hose and wash the plant down, being certain to hit both sides of the leaves. If the plant is in a pot, you can try swishing it in warm, soapy (not detergent) water. Use one tablespoon of soap to one gallon of water. Let it dry, then wash it again with plain, warm water to prevent any soap damage to the leaves. This treatment dislodges the mites and they will fall off. Since they're rather lazy critters, they usually

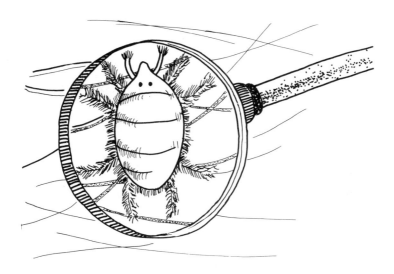

Figure 6-1. Red spider mite.

don't have the energy to climb back on. But because you might
not get them all the first time and there will probably be eggs to
contend with that will hatch later, the washing should be done
once a week for three to four weeks, depending on how bad the
infestation is. Of course, you could also use a systemic insecticide. *A what?* A systemic insecticide. This works by poisoning
the insect as it eats the insecticide-sprayed leaves. The nice thing
about a systemic is that it can't be washed off by rain or sprinkling since it is taken up by the plant and is in its cells. Another
plus is that the "good guys" like ladybugs and bees are safe
because they don't eat plants. If they sit on the leaves, they won't
be affected. Systemics also come in a granular form which is
sprinkled on the soil and watered in. If I use chemicals, I like to
use these because I feel there is less waste. When I spray, I usually
manage to cover everything within five feet of what needs the
chemical. With the high price of these gardening aids, I feel as if
I'm throwing money away.

   Aphids are easy critters to see on your plants because of their
size and the clusters they form. They come in a variety of colors—
green, black, red, white—and have plump, juicy, globular little
bodies (see Figure 6-2a and b). They exhibit a preference for
tender, succulent new growth or for flower buds. To say that
aphids are prolific is a gross understatement. Better fasten your

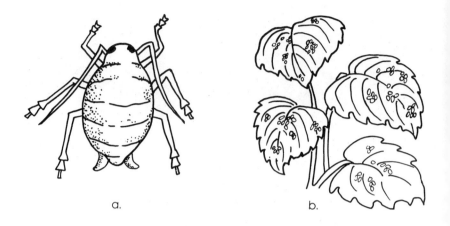

Figure 6-2 (a and b). Aphids.

seatbelts for this one. During the summer, a female aphid doesn't even need a male to get pregnant. As if that's not bad enough, during that time she can give birth to live females. If you think that's atrocious, wait until you hear this. These little live female aphids are already pregnant when they're born. How do we even stand a chance against those odds? Fortunately, however, you can get rid of them in the same way you do spider mites, just as long as you're persistent.

Do you have tiny cottony masses on the leaves and joints of your plants? Those are mealybugs. Often they first show up on

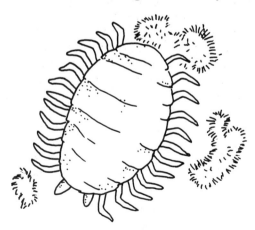

Figure 6-3. Mealy bug.

the undersides of leaves along the midrib (see Figure 6-3). They exude a sweet, sticky substance that sometimes attracts ants. As with spider mites, a good strong blast of water may dislodge some. After the plant has dried, use a cotton swab dipped in alcohol to touch each one that remains on the plant. They're usually large, and after the water treatment there shouldn't be too many left, so don't despair, it won't take all day. Keep an eye on the plant, and if you should notice new mealybugs, give them the alcohol treatment again. I told a friend of mine about this, and she later complained that the treatment didn't work. Upon investigation, I found that she was using brandy ("Well, it *is* alcohol," she said.) When I say alcohol, I mean rubbing alcohol. Again, a systemic insecticide will also do the trick, as will a contact chemical. Contact means that it kills the insect on contact. Some have a residual effect also—an insect that lands on a sprayed area will be killed if it is within a certain length of time. Of course, one problem with a contact chemical is that it will zap beneficial insects as well as pests.

I try to stay away from plants (yes, even free ones) with extremely bad infestations of any insects but particularly those with white flies. These insects are very mobile and can infest other plants in no time. So unless you want to use several applications of insecticide or have an area where you can isolate the plant, I would pass by these plants. White flies are about the size of fruit flies, are white (naturally), and have triangular wings (see Figure 6-4). They are attracted to bright yellow colors, so if you

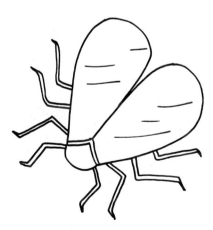

Figure 6-4. White fly.

care to take the time to paint a board that color and coat it with something sticky such as car oil, you can trap the little creatures. If a plant has spider mites or mealybugs, it shouldn't touch other plants. But if it has white flies, it must be isolated completely. If the infestation is not severe, dip or spray the plant with warm, soapy water once a week for three weeks. Then, if they're not too large, put the pot and plant in a plastic bag and keep the plant out of direct sunlight. That way, any flies that hatch will be caught in the bag and can be destroyed. This will also let you know when the infestation is over. If you find no white flies for five weeks, you can be fairly certain that no more eggs will hatch.

Do any of your plants have colonies of small, flat, or rounded "oyster shells" attached to the undersides of their leaves or along the stems? The problem, then, is probably scale insects. The shell part is a covering that protects the insect and makes it tough for a contact-type insecticide to work. You're better off going to a systemic if you choose to follow the chemical route. If not, if the individual scales are fairly large and there's only a few, you can flick them off with your fingernail—just be careful not to damage the tissues of the plant. Or, if they're on a woody stem, scrub them off gently with an old, soft toothbrush. If you find them on the larger trees and shrubs already in your landscape, you'll probably have to use a dormant oil spray in winter. Ask your local nursery owner what is recommended in your area (see Figure 6-5).

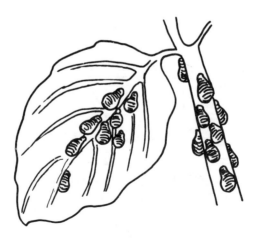

Figure 6-5. Scale.

In the part of the country where I live, slugs are a *big* problem. They seem to be prevalent on the bottoms of pots that come from a nursery. They have voracious appetites and can devastate a plant, eating big chunks out of the prettiest flowers and most succulent leaves in no time, especially if the plant is under the weather to begin with. Sometimes you'll even find their eggs in the soil. They are laid in a cluster and look like miniature pearls. Don't be finicky, squash them. As for the grown slugs, when I find them I step on them. There are some baits on the market that seem to work very well. I don't use them, however, because I have a dog who thinks they're the next best thing to filet mignon and I don't care to have a sick pup on my hands. So I handpick them. Slugs are night feeders and like to rest in dark moist places during the day. Put boards in your infirmary area and check under them often. This will help keep the slug population under control. Also pick up each pot and check the bottom and sides. I've also heard that setting a saucer of beer out will attract them and they'll drown. But beer is more expensive to use then boards, so you know which method I prefer.

IT'S FOR THE BIRDS

If you're really into natural control, start feeding the birds. For bugs in general, they're great. And they're free. (If you don't count bird food, that is. It's still cheaper than chemicals, though.) You can attract birds not only with food but also by providing housing, water, and killing the neighbor's cat. (Can you tell I've read *101 Things to do with a Dead Cat*?) Seriously though, hanging a feeder or nesting box near the plants that need protection will do wonders. Of course, you don't want to overfeed since then you'll be defeating your purpose. Remember that insect-eating birds prefer suet, peanut butter, and the like. But don't discourage seed-eaters. They will help your yard by eating weed seeds. Some of the best birds to have around are bluebirds, chickadees, mockingbirds, orioles, robins, wrens, and warblers. Yes, I know that some of them eat worms. But they make up for it by feasting on nasty critters too. Don't you occasionally eat something you shouldn't?

Then, of course, there are the predatory insects such as ladybugs and praying mantis. I've ordered them through the mail but have never had any luck at keeping them around—they seem to prefer my neighbor's yard, so I can't give much advice on them. Your best bet is to call the county agent and ask. You know, I feel sorry for him if you really do call as often as I suggest you do.

If you're going to bring any plants into your house from the infirmary, or from anywhere else outside for that matter, be prepared to battle the bugs for a while. They always seem to show up in droves about thirty days after I bring my plants inside. I guess that's because I water outside with a hose and probably spray off enough of the bugs to keep them under control. In the house, I make at least a half-hearted attempt to keep the water just on the soil and in the pot, so the bugs are free to multiply as they please.

An insect that frequently shows up in the house and is really more annoying than a threat to your plants is the fungus gnat. You'll usually see it fly up when you water. It looks just like a fruit fly but lives on decayed vegetable matter in the soil. With an extremely high population, some will start to eat the roots. To control this pest, a soil drench is often used. Ask where you buy your chemicals which one is best for this use. Another method is to repot the plant, removing all the soil from around the roots and replacing it with fresh soil. It's a good idea to wash the roots and plant too.

If you choose the chemical route, the process must be repeated in about two weeks because the larvae and adults will be killed but not the eggs. Mix the solution at half strength of whatever is recommended and pour it around the base of the plant, letting it soak into the soil. Cover the entire soil surface with enough of the mixture so that it drains out of the bottom of the pot. That's all there is to it. When you bring nonhardy plants in for the winter, it's a good idea to do this. On herbs, however, I don't use any chemicals at all. That's just my personal preference. Some products are labeled as safe to use on edible plants, but I just don't choose to use them unless it's a dire necessity. Something I've just heard about but haven't tried yet is using bleach. Mix one tablespoon with a gallon of water and drench the soil with it. According to a friend of mine who swears by this method, the bleach will kill all bugs in the soil. Remember, though, that it probably won't touch the eggs, so the process will have to be repeated.

IS IT CONTAGIOUS?

Diseases aren't usually a big problem in the house, but they can be in the infirmary. Literally hundreds of diseases await your plants, but the possibility of having a problem with more than one or two is slight unless you bring home a nursery's cast-off with some unusual malady. One of the problems I've run into most often as I've gardened across the country is powdery mildew. I've found that some of the most susceptible plants are dahlia (*Dahlia* various), garden forget-me-not (*Myosotis* various), lilac (*Syringa* various), phlox (*Phlox* various), and rose (*Rosa* various). Since the disease is spread by the wind, there isn't too much you can do to keep it out of your yard. How do you know if your plants have it? Look for a white or gray powdery or mealy coating on leaves, tender stems, and flower buds. If you see it on any of these, this means mildew (see Figure 6-6). Fungicides are on the market to spray infected plants, but these can run into money. Of course, anything over $1.98 a gallon is "spendy" to me. So if I have to buy it, I try to get several people together to share the cost (a quart goes a long way), or I try to buy it wholesale. As far as preventive methods are concerned, it's a good idea to water from below (like with a soaker hose); or, if you have to use an overhead watering system, do it early in the day so the leaves have a chance to dry before night. If you water with a hand-held hose, try not to splatter soil or mulch to avoid spreading the mildew. If the disease is not severe, don't worry too much about it. If it's covering the buds, it's time to panic and bring on the spray, as this could damage the plant's flower production.

Black spot is another fungus disease that often shows up on roses. The disease looks just like its name, although the spots usually start out yellow and then turn black, eventually causing

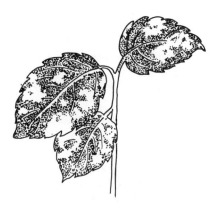

Figure 6-6. Powdery mildew.

Figure 6-7. Black spot.

the leaves to fall off (see Figure 6-7). In my infirmary, when I bring in a rose bush, it seems I'm fighting a constant battle with black spot. It overwinters on dead leaves under the plants, so if the bush is in a pot pick out all dead leaves and burn them. (Don't put them in the compost pile or you'll probably spread the problem.) Again, the expensive fungicides will help control it, but this method takes a constant spraying program to keep it completely out of the garden. If you're intent on growing a lot of roses and want them to keep all their leaves, either scrounge the resistant varieties (many of the newer ones have more resistance bred into them) or buy a good sprayer. Don't try to use a discarded spray bottle the way I did. One summer of that and my hand was in the permanent shape of one. Again, try to get a sprayer wholesale. If you have to order half a dozen to get one, see if you can interest neighbors or garden club members in buying the others. If you sell them at wholesale prices, you shouldn't have any trouble finding takers. The same watering advice goes for black spot as for powdery mildew. This will not stop it entirely but will hold it down somewhat.

There's a new product on the market that is an insecticidal soap. I got a free sample at the landscape convention I crashed. Upon reading the literature, I found that it is supposed to help control diseases as well as many insects.. And since it's a soap, it's not harmful to the environment.

It's not likely that insects and diseases will be a big problem in your infirmary, but because the plants there are under stress to begin with, they will recover more quickly if you can keep the problems under control. You can then move the plants more quickly into your landscape and create additional room for the other "sickies" I'm sure you'll be picking up.

7

The
Maternity Ward

Maternity

What happens if a person asks if you would like a cutting or some seeds rather than a whole plant? By all means, don't refuse just because you've never grown anything from cuttings or seeds. If you make an attempt and it doesn't work, you will have learned something and all you'll have spent is a little time. If they grow, you'll have acquired more plants for nothing and you'll have more self-confidence next time the situation arises.

If you're still skittish, think about this, using a chrysanthemum as an example. If you get one free cutting and root it, you have one free plant. Then if you take cuttings of your original plant, you can get dozens—and you haven't spent a dime on them. The same goes for seeds, only more so. Someone gives you, say, two dozen perennial candytuft seeds. Even if only half of these germinate and of those only half survive, you still end up with six free candytufts. And do you know how many seeds those six plants will produce? Hundreds! Take it from me, you'll be able to supply the neighborhood.

If I still haven't convinced you, how about considering it a kid's project. You can pawn off the work of planting and watering on them, and then put the blame on them if they don't grow. It will be a "growing" experience for all involved.

Okay, say I've talked you into it. Now what? Brace yourself. It's time for you to learn the various propagation techniques. Many of them are ridiculously easy; some of them aren't. Most gardeners don't need to know more than a few of the basics, however, so don't panic, because it's not going to be much of a trauma for you at all.

One of the easiest, quickest, and most reliable methods is called *plant division*. The list of plants that can be divided goes on and on. Just to give you an idea, here are a few: aster (*Aster* various), chrysanthemum (*Chrysanthemum* various), daylily (*Hemerocallis* various), black-eyed Susan (*Rudbeckia hirta*), speedwell (*Veronica* various), and yarrow (*Achillea* various).

Of course, you're going to run into some plants for which this method won't work well. Some, like peony (*Paeonia* various), don't like their roots disturbed, and others such as lupine (*Lupinus* various) and hollyhock (*Alcea rosea*) have a taproot like a carrot that makes this method difficult. Some plants that have fleshy roots such as plantain lily (*Hosta* various) and astilbe (*Astilbe* various) can be divided this way as long as the roots are not allowed to dry out and are dusted with a fungicide before replanting to prevent rot.

Early spring is the best time to divide plants just as they're starting to grow and right after they're through flowering. To begin, dig up the entire plant, prune it to about four inches tall, then shake off as much soil as possible without injuring the roots. Plants such as some primrose (*Primula* various), bellflower (*Campanula* various), and aubrieta (*Aubrieta deltoidea*) have crowns that naturally separate the parent plant into individual new plantlets. When you dig plants such as these, you will actually be able to see the divisions. Insert a sharp knife or spade into the space between the divisions and cut apart. Sometimes the roots may be so loosely intertwined that it's possible simply to pull them into separate clumps with your hands. Others, like daylily (*Hemerocallis* various), have roots that are so tough and intertwined that it may be necessary to insert two garden forks back to back in the center of the clump and pry the sections apart (see Figures 7-1a, b, and c). Don't feel badly about being rather rough in a case like this. Daylilies are tough and can take quite a bit of abuse.

Just make certain that whichever way you do it, you end up with roots on each piece. No roots equals a dead plant.

If you find a woody area in the center of the clump, discard it, because it won't perform well if replanted. This is the original parent plant and is probably all worn out.

Once the plants have been divided into sections, just plant them as you would any clump of the plant, and water well.

Now, isn't that a fast, easy, inexpensive method? And you can use it on lots of plants.

Another method is called *layering*. This is also easy because the branch that is being propagated is sustained by the parent with water and minerals while it is rooting and therefore goes through a minimum of trauma. The only disadvantage with this method is that it takes a while to produce a good-sized new plant.

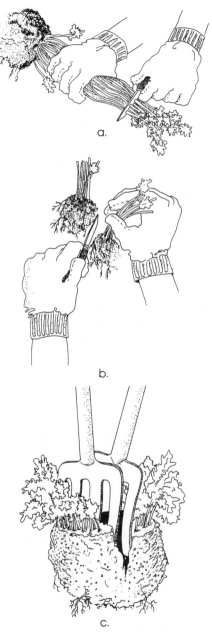

Figure 7-1 (a,b,c). Division.

To layer a plant, loosen the soil next to the plant with a fork or hand trowel. Dig a trench about four inches deep and a foot long. Pick the branch that you would like to become your new plant. It should be about eighteen inches long. Do not remove it from the parent plant; just take off any leaves or side shoots for about the first foot, starting where it joins the parent. Leave the last six inches toward the tip with the leaves on. Then simply bend the branch down and pin it into the trench with a bent wire or horseshoe nail. Make the branch take a sharp bend upwards just before the leafy section and cover the leafless part with soil to a depth of about four inches. If you don't have wire or nails, you can cover the branch with soil and then put a rock or brick on top of it to hold the branch in place. Water at this time and also during any dry periods (see Figure 7-2a, b, and c).

When new growth starts at the tip, it generally means that roots have formed. Sever the branch from the parent plant with a sharp knife or pruning shears but leave the new plant in place for several weeks so it can get established on its own. Then you can transplant it.

The amount of time that a plant will take to layer depends on factors such as moisture, heat, and the type of plant it is. Layering can take anywhere from two months to a year, so be patient. If your soil is very hard or clayey, add sand and peat to the trench to loosen the soil and hasten rooting. Good drainage is important too, since the branch will have a tendency to rot if left in soggy soil.

The best time to start layering is in late winter or early spring. This gives the plant a head start on hot, dry weather. Try to use a young branch since it is usually more bendable.

If you have a shrub that is very woody, you may need to wound it to get it to produce roots. To do this, make a slit about halfway through the stem at the angle where the branch will start to come up off the bottom of the trench. Insert a pebble or match stick into it to hold it open. Then proceed as with nonwoody plants.

Some of the many plants that you can propagate using the layering method are: azalea (*Rhododendron* various), climbing rose (*Rosa* various), euonymus (*Euonymus* various), garland daphne (*Daphne cneorum*), Japanese spurge (*Pachysandra terminalis*), and vervain (*Verbena* various).

a.

b.

c.

Figure 7-2 (a,b,c). Layering.

Other plants, such as strawberry geranium (*Saxifraga stolonifera*), carpet bugle (*Ajuga* various), Indian mock strawberry (*Duchesnea indica*), and beach strawberry (*Fragaria chiloensis*), will layer by themselves.

Stem cuttings are a bit more difficult to do than the other two methods I've discussed. This is because you completely sever a piece of the plant from the parent and try to convince it to produce its own roots. Since this way is not as foolproof as the other methods, it's best to take several cuttings of the plant you would like, just in case they all don't survive.

Stem cuttings can be made in three different ways. The easiest one is called a *softwood cutting*. Many houseplants, lilac (*Syringa* various), buttercup winter hazel (*Corylopsis pauciflora*), Warminster broom (*Cytisus praecox*), lily-of-the-valley bush (*Pieris japonica*), azalea (*Rhododendron* various), and arrowwood (*Viburnum* various) can be propagated in this manner.

In the early morning, when the plant is full of moisture, choose a stem, preferably one without flower buds, and cut it off with a sharp knife to a length of two to six inches. If you have a choice of taking a piece from a sunny or shady location, choose the one from the sun. There is a better chance that it is healthier and therefore will root more easily. This tip pertains to all the types of stem cuttings I'll discuss.

Make the cut just below a node, the place on the stem where the leaves come out. Usually there is a bump, ridge, or line that marks it. With most plants, the roots will develop here, so it's imperative to have at least two and preferably five nodes on the cutting. Remove the leaves from the lower two-thirds of the branch and dip the cut end in a rooting hormone. Besides helping a plant to root more easily, these hormones often contain a fungicide that helps to prevent the cutting from rotting before it can root.

Now your cutting is ready to pot. You can use vermiculite, sand, or perlite, whichever you have on hand. Some gardeners are certain that they have more success with one over the other, but I haven't found any noticeable difference. I use sterile pots that I've cleaned with a stiff brush and soaked in a solution of one tablespoon of bleach and a gallon of hot water. After wetting the medium, take a pencil or stick and make holes in it for the cuttings. Insert the cutting, placing at least two of the nodes and preferably three below the level of the medium. Tamp the medium

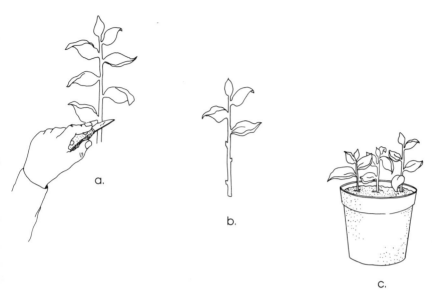

Figure 7-3 (a,b,c). Stem cutting for softwoods.

down around the cuttings and water again. Place them in a spot where they will receive indirect light. They may wilt a little the first day or two, but they should recover after that. Keep an eye open for mildew or fungus, and if you should see even a hint, spray with a fungicide. Within two to six weeks, you should have rooted cuttings to plant. These will be rather tender, so when you plant them, give them extra attention—perhaps some light shade to begin with if you are planting them in the sun (see Figure 7-3a, b, and c).

When you take a softwood cutting of geranium (*Pelargonium* various) or any other plant that has milky juice in its stem, expose the cutting to the air (but not to the sun) for twenty-four to thirty-six hours. This will promote the formation of a callus and help to prevent rot. Then proceed as with any other softwood cutting.

Another type of stem cutting is the *semi-hardwood cutting*. This one is taken in summer or early fall. The cuttings themselves are older than softwood but not quite mature. You can tell that they're semi-hardwood when the cuttings snap instead of bend. Take the cuttings in exactly the same way you did the softwood and treat and pot them in the same way. Here's where the sim-

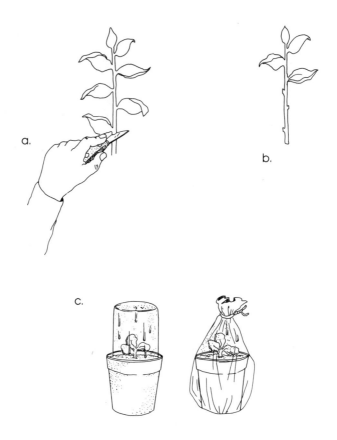

Figure 7-4 (a,b,c). Stem cutting for semi-hardwoods.

ilarity ends. Rather than leaving them exposed outside, keep the cuttings more humid and warm. They need to stay at a temperature above 40° F. A cold frame works well for this. Some people use a cold frame and equip it with heating cables. This makes it a warm frame, but I'm too cheap to spend the money on cables and electricity to run them, so I just take more cuttings and use my cold frame. (see Figure 7-4a, b, and c).

Plants that propagate well from semihardwood cuttings are: hydrangea (*Hydrangea* various), rose (*Rosa* various), firethorn (*Pyracantha* various), cotoneaster (*Cotoneaster* various), wild lilac (*Ceanothus sanguineus*), salal (*Gaultheria shallon*), juniper

(*Juniperus* various), arborvitae (*Thuja* various), hemlock (*Tsuga* various), gardenia (*Gardenia* various), holly (*Ilex* various), spindle tree (*Euonymus* various), and pittosporum (*Pittosporum* various).

The third type of cutting is a *hardwood cutting*. I'll tell you right up front that I think it's a hassle and I just plain don't do it anymore. It can take up to two years to produce a rooted cutting by this method, and I'm not that patient a person. But just in case you really want to try it, I'll tell you how.

Take cuttings any time from fall to spring from the leafless stems of the dormant growth of last year's new growth. (If that doesn't confuse and discourage you, nothing will—so you'll probably have fantastic success with this method.) Take the cuttings from the middle of the stems, discarding the tips. Just remember which end is up when you cut off the tips. Each cutting should be one-quarter to one inch in diameter, seven to ten inches long, and contain three nodes. Place these pieces horizontally into sand or aged sawdust and keep them through the winter as close as possible to 45° F. Again, a cold frame is a good place. During the winter, a callus will form on the cut ends. In the spring, plant the cuttings (right side up, of course) so that just the tip shows above the soil. Then wait and wait and wait. Eventually, you might get a plant (see Figure 7-5a and b).

If you live in a part of the country with fairly warm winters, you can put the cutting directly into the soil. Dig a hole and put one inch of sand in the bottom for drainage. Then insert the cutting vertically and bury half its length. Use good soil to fill in with, and keep it moist throughout the year.

Privet (*Ligustrum* various), wisteria (*Wisteria* various), grape (*Vitis* various), flowering quince (*Chaenomeles* various), poplar (*Populus* various), and mulberry (*Morus* various), for example, should root using this method.

Root cuttings are fairly easy to take. It's nice to know how to use this method because if you see someone transplanting a plant you'd like and they don't want to give you a division, or the plant doesn't lend itself to division, you can simply ask for a few pieces of root. Most gardeners won't mind letting you have them, especially if you sound like you know what you're doing. You can take root cuttings of bleeding heart (*Dicentra* various), oriental poppy (*Papaver orientale*), plumbago (*Ceratostigma* various), summer phlox (*Phlox paniculata*), bayberry (*Myrica pen-*

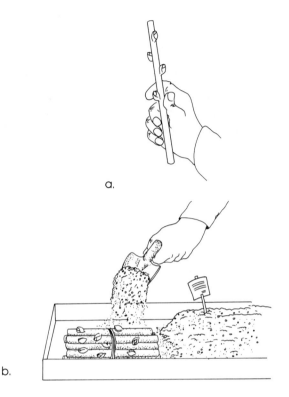

Figure 7-5 (a and b). Taking hardwood cuttings.

sylvanica), rose acacia (*Robinia hispida*), bottlebrush buckeye (*Aesculus parviflora*), Japanese pagoda tree (*Sophora japonica*), sumac (*Rhus* various), quaking aspen (*Populus tremuloides*), varnish tree (*Koelreuteria paniculata*), passionflower (*Passiflora* various), and trumpet creeper (*Campsis* various). That ought to be enough to get your landscaping started.

In late winter or early spring, dig up a plant and cut two- to four-inch pieces from young roots. The finer the root, the longer the piece should be. Prune the top of the plant to compensate for the root loss. Also remember which end is up. The top is the end that is nearest to the crown of the plant. Remove the little side roots that protrude and put the cutting either directly into the ground or into a pot, top end up. In either case, the soil should be very sandy and loose. Keep the top end just level with the surface of the soil. Then put one inch of plain sand over it and water. Don't take too many cuttings at once because they should not be exposed to the air for any length of time. Have everything you're

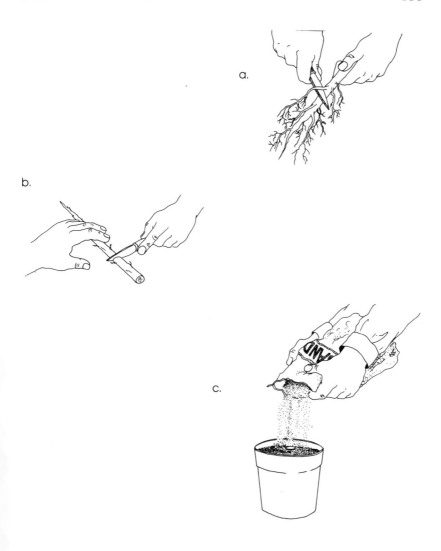

Figure 7-6 (a,b,c). Root cutting.

going to need prepared ahead of the time you take the cutting and work quickly (see Figure 7-6a, b, and c).

Take a bigger cutting if you're going to put it directly into the ground. And whatever you do, don't use a rooting hormone on the cutting. This doesn't work and may actually inhibit growth. However, you can dust the cutting with a fungicide to help prevent rot.

In a cold frame, it will take about eight weeks to produce the start of a new plant. In the ground, it can take up to sixteen weeks.

I really don't want to talk about *grafting*, but since the editor "suggested" that I supply information on the process, I thought I'd pass on to you what my experiences were. I've taken two classes devoted exclusively to grafting. In each one, I diligently took notes and paid attention. In every lab that followed, I practiced what I had learned. Out of all the grafts I tried, and there were several of each type of graft, not one, I repeat, not a single one took. I am a failure at grafting. I firmly believe you either have the knack or you don't. I am loathe to admit it, but I definitely don't. Knowing the sordid details, I'm sure both the reader and my editor now will excuse me from further discussing the subject. If you really want to give it a try—if you are dying to graft a fruit tree, one of those fantastic red cutleaf Japanese maples (*Acer palmatum* various), or a tree rose—take a class or get one of the books dealing specifically with the subject.

If anyone is asking "Why bother to graft?" there are several reasons. Perhaps you have an apple tree that bears a type of apple you're not fond of. Instead of taking it out and starting with a new, young plant, you can simply (ha! for me, not so simply) graft on a branch from a variety of apple you like. Or even several varieties. In the case of roses, you can graft a tender rose on top of a very cold-resistant rose root and produce one that will survive in colder climates. You can even make your own tree roses. So, you see, there are uses for it. I'm just not coordinated enough to make it work for me.

A BULB BY ANY OTHER NAME . . .

The propagation of bulbs is really quite simple. Technically, this section will deal with the propagation of bulbs, tubers, rhizomes, pips, and corms. Sound confusing? They are all similar, yet different, but I don't think it's necessary for the casual gardener to know all the technicalities of these differences. Whatever they are called, you can make it easier on yourself by just thinking of them as a form of bulb. So if I say "divide the pip," just substitute the word "bulb" for "pip" and you'll know what I mean.

It's amazing what good bulbs people will discard or be willing to give away. These can be propagated and easily incorporated into your landscape (see Figure 7-7).

Figure 7-7. A flowering border using bulbs commonly found discarded (*Jane Kailing*).

Here are some of the bulbs you will most commonly find in alleyways or perhaps see growing in people's yards and be able to work a trade for. Keep in mind that this is in no way a complete list and that there are many ways to propagate some of them. I have described what I believe to be the easiest propagating methods for the home gardener.

Achimenes (*Achimenes patens*) have small, tender, perennial rhizomes that look like little scale-covered cones. Since they are not hardy and have to be grown in pots, you'll rarely "find" them, but do buy some (at wholesale) because they're certainly worth the price. They produce tubular flowers in pink, blue, and purple and add nice spots of color to shady areas. Once you have a pot planted, after it has flowered and the foliage has died back, you can carefully sift through the soil, find the original rhizomes, and break off the new baby rhizomes to start another pot. Over the winter, store them in a cool, dry place and repot them in the spring.

Amaryllis (*Hippeastrum* various) bulbs are hardy only in warm winter areas, but they are fun to grow anywhere in pots. If you know anyone who works in a hospital, ask them to look for the bulbs for you. Often they'll be discarded by patients who don't want to bother with them when they go home. They can be propagated by separating the little bulblets that may form on the side of the original bulb in early spring or late summer.

Autumn crocus (*Colchicum autumnale*) is also called meadow saffron. This corm is really not a crocus at all, but is a member of the lily family. It brings hard-to-find pink, rose-purple, or white color in the fall. Since the flower appears after the foliage has died down, it looks best to plant them in a ground cover so they don't look so "undressed." I've got mine surrounded by violets. Little cormels can be removed from the parent corms after the foliage dies in summer.

Canna (*Canna* various) are tuberous rootstocks that are hardy in all but the coldest zones. They are an old-fashioned plant with a tropical look and come in a wide variety of colors and sizes. Some of the new dwarf varieties are especially desirable. Divide the rhizomes in the spring.

Crocus (*Crocus* various) corms can sometimes be found discarded in large masses. Many flower colors and sizes are available, but all produce grass-like foliage. They are one of the earliest spring-blooming bulbs. Remove the young corms from the parent corms after the foliage has died.

Dahlia (*Dahlia* various) tubers come in all sizes from the tiny border dahlias (which will bloom from seed in one year) to the giant eight-foot-tall dinner plate dahlias. People who grow them always seem to have an overabundance of tubers as the plants multiply so quickly. Since many are large plants, the gardener soon runs out of room and so is often more than happy to share. Divide the tubers in the fall, taking an eye (the growing point—like the eye of a potato) with each piece.

Daffodil (*Narcissus* various) bulbs are one of the most common bulbs I find discarded. There are literally hundreds of varieties available. Who knows which one you'll find cast out? Maybe it will be the old standard yellow, 'King Alfred,' but perhaps not. Offset bulbs may be separated from the parent bulb every couple of years.

Freesia (*Freesia* various) is another tender corm but one so deliciously fragrant that it's worth the trouble to keep it in a pot. It's only hardy in warm winter areas. They will often bloom from seed about nine months after planting.

Gladiolus (*Gladiolus* various) corms produce flowers that are superb for cutting. Since in many areas they must be dug and stored during winter, often they are found discarded because people tire of this chore. Some of the shorter varieties are especially nice in the garden since they don't require staking to keep them upright. Little cormels form on the sides of the parent corm and can be removed when the plants are dug, and be planted in the spring.

Grape hyacinth (*Muscari* various) produces little bulbs that are very prolific multipliers. Almost anyone who has them in their garden shouldn't mind digging up a clump for you. Besides the purple and blue varieties, there is one with an attractive white flower. When bulbs become crowded, they may be lifted and the clump may be divided.

Hardy cyclamen (*Cyclamen* various) is a tuberous rooted plant that comes in a variety of pinks, reds, and white. It makes a charming ground cover in a shady spot. They may be propagated by seed.

Hyacinth (*Hyacinthus orientalis*) bulbs will perform their best in cold winter climates. They get extra points in my book for their fantastic fragrance. After several years in the ground, one bulb will form a clump that may be lifted and divided.

Iris (*Iris* various) experts claim that over two hundred species of this plant exist. Except for the unusual varieties, most gardeners who have them are more than willing to share as they multiply so quickly. From July through September, divide the rhizomes by cutting them with a sharp knife. Discard the old woody center section and replant the rest.

Lily (*Lilium* various) bulbs often produce wonderfully fragrant flowers. You'll find a variety of different scents, not only the heavy one associated with Easter lilies. Watch for gardeners digging and dividing their clumps in the fall, or remove the bulbils that form in the leaf axils.

Lily-of-the-valley (*Convallaria majalis*) is a pip that produces a fragrant white (or sometimes pink) bell-shaped flower. It makes a good ground cover in the shade. After the foliage has died down in the fall, dig the clumps and separate them.

Mexican shell flower (*Tigridia pavonia*) is a bulb that can be left in the ground only in mild winter areas, but the flowers are so unusual and are such show stoppers that they're worth the extra effort. Since very few gardeners have them, don't bother trying to find them. They are easily grown from seed and may bloom the first year after planting.

Ornamental onion (*Allium* various) is a bulb that is related to the edible onion. Over four hundred species are available, many of which are pleasantly fragrant. They make wonderful cut flowers and also dry very well. Separate the little bulblets from the base of the parent bulb in early fall.

Tuberous begonia (*Begonia* various) is another plant that is not hardy in most places, but it is worth the effort to grow the tubers in pots because of the outstanding color they produce in shady places. These are often sold by florists as gifts, so ask your friends to save them for you if they receive any. Divide the tubers in early spring after the eyes begin to develop.

Tulip (*Tulipa* various) is another bulb that does best in cold winter climates. The varieties available are fantastic—from the tiny botanical species to the tall, stately emperors. Other than by the size of the bulb (and that's not always a reliable factor), it's hard to tell one variety from another. After the foliage has died back, detach the offset bulbs.

Windflower (*Anenome* various) tubers produce flowers in a wide selection of colors. They are excellent for cutting. Lift the clumps in late summer and divide them.

You can also go the the library for information on propagation. (By this time, you should be intimately familiar with the gardening section.) Books on how to start plants from seeds, cuttings, ground layering, air layering, grafting, and much more are abundant. Be sure to scan through the books, however, since some are geared for the more advanced gardener and contain terminology that you might find confusing or difficult to understand. But more and more books are being written for the novice, and they are usually accompanied by pictures and drawings to clarify points that might otherwise be misunderstood.

Don't forget your friendly county agent. Many counties have a special home gardening or horticultural person who usually has a wealth of knowledge available on plant propagation. These specialists will be happy to send you brochures and pamphlets on both general gardening topics and specific subjects you inquire about. And yes, many are free, although some I have requested cost ten to twenty-five cents. The best thing about this information is that it's geared to your locale. Do you want to know the best way to propagate roses? You don't have to wade through pages telling you how it's done in Nova Scotia or Baja California. You won't have to wonder if the directions apply to your area. Get the information from the county agent and you'll know.

Now back to the seed or cutting that's in your hand. Of course, if it's summer, you may want to sow the seeds directly into the ground or place the cutting right in the bed where you want it to grow. I've had great success growing seeds this way but no luck at all using this method with cuttings. I know many people who do it and make it work, but I don't know the secret. One woman gave me a dozen assorted fuschia cuttings and explicit directions on how to put them directly into the garden to root. Every single one of them died. Sheepishly, I went back, asked for more, got them, and all twelve of them lived. The second time I rooted them in the house in vermiculite. My rule of thumb is this: If I get only one cutting of a variety, I start it in the house. If I get two but they're unusual or hard to get, I still start them in the house. If I get two or more and they're more common, I try half outside and half inside.

A HOLE IN THE SIDE IS WORTH TWO IN THE BOTTOM

Let's assume that you're going to start the seeds or cuttings in your house. I have a tendency to overwater my houseplants and usually do it with seeds and cuttings too. Remember what I said earlier about putting holes in both the bottom and sides of the containers? This is a particular must if you are an overwaterer. I must admit, however, that one of my friends never puts any holes at all in her containers and grows gorgeous plants from seed. Of course, she's the type who could grow tropical orchids in Siberia too. But as for me, I would rather be safe than sorry, so I punch lots of holes both in the bottom and lower sides.

I put the "holey" containers on old cookie sheets or in cake pans so they don't drip on my furniture and so I can water from the bottom (I'll get into that later). Use your imagination and you will be surprised at your own inventiveness. I've used everything from plastic milk jugs cut in half to egg cartons for growing plants. As long as the item is clean and has holes, it really doesn't matter what you use. Just don't try to start seeds of large plants such as tomatoes in egg cartons unless you're prepared to transplant them several times. Use those to start little plants—say, leaf lettuce. Once you let people know what you're doing, they'll be more than happy to save things for you to use. You can even promise to reward them with a plant when they make some contribution. One of the occupational hazards of being a pennypincher and a seed grower is that you generally plant quite a number of seeds just in case some don't survive. Then if they all do survive, you can't throw the extras away and you're stuck with a lot more plants than you need. By giving these leftovers to friends, you move high on their lists and often are remembered when they have plants to dispose of, when they know of someone else who has, or when they have extra milk cartons.

A good medium to start both cuttings and seeds is vermiculite because it's inexpensive, light in weight, and sterile. However, I will use anything that is free or very, very inexpensive. One of my neighbors works for a cement company and occasionally brings me buckets of free sand. The drawback is that it's not sterile and is mighty heavy. The advantage is that it's free. I sterilize it in my oven and plant away. How do you sterilize potting medium? Several methods are practical in the home. One way is to dampen the medium slightly and spread it less than four inches deep in shallow pans. Place them in an oven preheated to 180° F. for two hours, then cool and store it in a covered container. One word of warning about using this method with soil: Some find the "fragrance" of baking soil objectionable. I don't. If you do, try this alternate method. Prepare the soil in the same manner but cover the pans with foil and seal the edges tightly. Pierce a hole in the center of the foil and insert a cooking thermometer into the soil, not allowing it to touch the pan. Heat the soil until the temperature reaches 180° F. and hold it there for thirty minutes. Do not remove the cover until the soil has cooled, then store it in the same way.

A quicker but messier method involves boiling water. Just put dry soil in flats that have holes in their bottoms and saturate them with two or three applications of boiling water. For obvious reasons, this is best performed outside. Allow the soil to dry and store.

Here's a method using a pressure cooker. Put two cups of water in the cooker. Place the rack inside and stack shallow pans of soil (about three-quarters of an inch deep) on the rack. Leave space between the pans for steam to circulate. Then turn on the heat and when the gauge reaches ten pounds of pressure, maintain it for fifteen minutes. Remove the cooker from the heat and allow it to cool before removing the lid. Store it in the same manner.

I've even read about a way to do it in the microwave but unfortunately can't remember where I saw the article. I called a local microwave cooking school but they couldn't help me. If any of you readers know where I might find the information, I'd sure appreciate hearing about it.

TO DIE OR NOT TO DIE

Having a sterile medium is very important because young seedlings have a tendency to "damp off" if it's not. Damp-off is a disease caused by a fungus. This fungus is always present, but it doesn't multiply fast enough to do much damage unless there is too much moisture, poor air circulation, or the growing medium is not sterile. It doesn't give you much warning either. Look at the seedlings one night and they're fine. The next morning they might all have toppled over at the shoot base. Then you know they've damped off, but it's also too late to do anything. That's why it's so important to have good drainage in your containers. Watering from the top in the evening also helps intensify this problem. The plants don't have time to dry off before it gets dark and cool and the fungus loves this. So water early in the day from the bottom. That means putting water in the bottom container (the one without holes) and letting the medium become moist from the bottom. When you touch the top of the medium and it's moist, you should remove the water remaining in the bottom container. This usually takes less than an hour.

Damping off is not such a great problem with cuttings since they are sturdier, but it does happen. However, overwatering is still something that should be avoided, and it's a good idea to bottom water cuttings too. Don't panic if a few of the lower leaves turn yellow. Just cut or break them off even with the stem and throw them out. And for heaven's sake, don't throw out the medium once your plants have rooted or seeds have sprouted and you've moved them into your garden. Medium can be resterilized and used again. Again, "A penny is a penny," as my mother said. I believe that old adage holds true even if the medium was free to begin with.

ONE GOOD CUTTING DESERVES ANOTHER

I take cuttings of many annuals and carry them over the winter in my house. I've had success with fibrous begonia (*Begonia semperflorens-cultorum*), coleus (*Coleus hybridus*), impatiens (*Impatiens wallerana*), geranium (*Pelargonium hortorum*), fuchsia (*Fuchsia* various), heliotrope (*Heliotropium arborescens*), and scented geranium (*Pelargonium* various). If you have room, the entire plant can be carried over. Unfortunately, my house isn't big enough to afford me the luxury of having a lot of potted plants inside over the winter. For those of you who don't want to attempt rooting cuttings in sterile medium, I've had success starting all these types of cuttings in water. I use yogurt cups (no holes this time), but anything at all is acceptable as long as it's clean. I fill them with lukewarm water, add about a half teaspoon of charcoal, and plop in the cuttings. Don't use the kind of charcoal you grill over. Remember the kind I told you to use to pulverize and dust on cactus and succulents? That's what you use, but don't pulverize it. And be certain that there are no leaves beneath the surface of the water. The leaves will make the water smelly and yucky when they start to deteriorate and won't help the cutting to root. If the water starts to look dirty before the cuttings have rooted, I throw it out and use fresh. I have kept rooted cuttings in water all winter, but it's better to pot them into regular house plant soil after they have rooted. The longer they are in water, the harder it is for them to acclimate to the soil, the bigger the shock will be, and the more probability there is that they will not survive. Don't wait until the roots are six inches long to put them into soil, either. Again, this will be a shock and the chances of the plant adapting to the soil medium are much less. I pot them up when the roots are only about one inch long.

One other hint: Always take more cuttings than you want because you don't know for sure that all of them will survive. Even if you treat all of them the same, some will make it and some won't. Besides, you can always use the extras for trading stock.

One of the most common mistakes made by people just getting started with growing plants from cuttings is that they try to start pieces that are too large. I find that larger cuttings have a higher mortality rate, take longer to root, and take up more room. If you are lucky enough to have a greenhouse, that's not such a problem. I use my laundry room, which is about the size of a pay toilet, so I don't have room for many cuttings or seedlings. But it's warm and moist, two conditions most seeds and cuttings love.

You'll find that many books mention using bottom heat to help cuttings root. These are special waterproof cables that you can buy especially for this purpose, but they are *very* expensive. Instead of purchasing these, I have used such diverse items as a yogurt maker and an old electric blanket covered with a sheet of plastic and set on low. I've also germinated seeds on top of my water heater and furnace. Just make sure that whatever you use is barely warm. You want to grow your seeds, not cook them. Generally, I use bottom heat only in the winter when I'm growing seed to get an early spring start. The water heater in the laundry keeps the room quite warm and the washer and dryer help contribute to the humidity. Speaking of humidity, if you live in a very dry climate or you're starting seeds in winter, cover them as soon as you plant them and for about two weeks after. Cover cuttings too—the percent that root will increase. Many books recommend glass, but that's expensive and, besides, I'm certain I'd break it. I use plastic (baggies for small things, dry cleaning bags for larger) and keep it from touching any leaves by making a tent with the help of a coat hanger.

Another reason I prefer plastic to glass is that when it comes time to remove the plastic to toughen up the plants before they're moved outdoors, rather than removing it all at once and shocking the plants, I punch holes in it to let more of the outside atmosphere in. Each day I punch a few more holes until there are more holes than plastic. Then I remove it entirely.

Don't put seedlings in direct sunlight—even if you're growing sun-loving cactus. That goes for cuttings too. They don't have any roots to take up water, so if you put them in the sun, they'll probably wilt in a mighty big hurry.

Once the seeds have germinated or cuttings have roots and you have removed the plastic, you can move them to partial sun for a couple of weeks, and then and only then into full sun. Naturally, if you have a shade-loving plant, never put it in the sun. Finally, if the weather is warm enough, you can move the plants into your garden. Of course, a lot depends on the type of seed you're growing. The smaller the seedling, the longer it needs extra protection. If it looks frail, don't subject it to the rigors of the outdoors so soon.

LIVE AND LEARN

How do you tell when a cutting has rooted? Easy. Take hold of the lowest set of leaves and gently (gently, I said), exert upward pressure. *Never* pull it up by the stem. All the cutting's health and well-being depend on what goes up and down within its stem, so if it is pinched or bruised even slightly, the chances of it surviving become less. If you find slight resistance, give it another week. If it appears that you would be able to tug quite hard without dislodging it, it probably has a fine root system. Of course, exceptions are found. When I was a beginning gardener, I took cuttings to root from several miniature roses. A week later, because I was anxious, I began to test the cuttings for roots. They resisted me quite strongly. I was amazed and pleased, congratulated myself on my ability, and proceeded to knock one out of its pot. Much to my chagrin, I found that it wasn't the roots that were creating the resistance, it was the thorns that were sticking out and preventing me from pulling the cutting out. Live and learn.

Some people swear by a rooting hormone; others swear at it. A rooting hormone is lightly dusted on the end of a cutting and is supposed to make it root faster. I've read an article or two that claimed that it inhibited root growth if used too liberally. I guess this is as much a question as whether chicken soup really cures a cold. Some hormones also contain a fungicide that helps prevent rot. I'll leave the decision up to you. Try it and come to your own conclusions. Oh yes, the containers don't carry this message, but hormones remain effective longer if kept cool and dry—like tightly capped in the refrigerator. Just warn your family that it's not some new kind of popcorn topping.

A SEED IN THE HAND . . .

When you receive seeds, ask if the donor has noticed lots of baby plants coming up in the vicinity of the parent. This will give you a clue that the plant is self-seeding. Many plants that are considered annual (only live for one year) will self-seed. That is, this year's plant dies, but the seeds that it produces will drop to the ground when ripe and come up again next year, etc., etc., ad infinitum. So each year you'll get more. When you get seeds like this, you can just sprinkle them on the ground where you want them to come up next year and perhaps dust a light covering of soil over them to hold them in place and water.

Each part of the country has its own selection of plants that self-seed. Some of these plants are on my dislike list because they self-seed so readily that they can become a nuisance. I seem to spend as much time pulling up these seedlings as pulling weeds.

An important point to remember is that the harsher the climate, such as very cold or dry, the harder it will be for a plant to self-seed. But if it is truly a rampant self-seeder, it will probably succeed to some degree almost anywhere.

Some self-seeders you might run across include: globe candytuft (*Iberis umbellata*), annual poinsettia (*Euphorbia heterophylla*), annual woodruff (*Asperula orientalis*), burning bush (*Kochia scoparia trichophylla*), California poppy (*Eschscholzia californica*), canterbury bells (*Campanula medium*), Chinese forget-me-not (*Cynoglossum amabile*), columbine (*Aquilegia* various), flower-of-an-hour (*Hibiscus trionum*), common foxglove (*Digitalis purpurea*), gloriosa daisy (*Rudbeckia hirta* 'gloriosa'), hollyhock (*Alcea rosea*), Johnny jump-up (*Viola tricolor*), larkspur (*Consolida ambigua*), moss rose (*Portulaca grandiflora*), stock (*Matthiola incana*), sweet alyssum (*Lobularia maritima*), and garden forget-me-not (*Myosotis sylvatica*). If in doubt, check the local library or county agent.

When you know which ones self-seed, you can include a small pair of scissors or a knife to your kit when you take a walk. If you see something in a yard that you want and it has gone to seed, knock on the door and ask permission to take some of the seed. I've done this many times and have never been turned down.

If you don't want a self-sower to crowd out your other plants, cut off the dying flowers before they make seeds. By the way, to tell if most kinds of seeds are ripe, crinkle a seedpod in your fingers. If it's dry, papery, and brownish and the seeds are hard, chances are the seeds are ready. If there are any green or moist parts, they're probably not.

To store seeds over winter (if you collect in the fall for spring planting), thoroughly dry them and place them in small paper bags or envelopes with a label identifying name, height, color, and perhaps which exposure they do best in. I put all my bags into a mason jar with a tight-fitting cover and place them on a rear shelf in the refrigerator. I don't even bother to start these types in the house. I just scatter them in the beds where I want them, cover them with a tad of soil, tamp them in, water, and wait. What could be easier—or cheaper?

When I get more seeds than I need, I share them with friends. I've used seeds as an easy, inexpensive little gift to send inside of letters to friends and relatives who are scattered throughout the country. I even trade with people when I have to buy a packet of seeds in order to get the variety I want. I almost always get more than I need in a packet, so rather than saving them for next year, I trade. Some friends and I have a type of informal seed exchange going. I've received some very unusual varieties in the mail from other parts of the country. Before you do this, however, find out if there are any restrictions in your state on sending seeds through the mail. A call to your state's department of agriculture should put you in touch with someone who can answer your questions. Much depends upon what kind of seed it is and where it's going. And, of course, a lot depends on your honesty. If you send a dozen hollyhock (*Alcea rosea*) seeds in a card to your grandmother in Illinois, I'm sure the Postal Service is not going to spot them and turn you in. But you wouldn't want to be responsible for starting a problem in another part of the country, would you? So check it out before you send.

One caution on collecting seeds. Today many plants are hybrids. This means that they may be sterile or the plants you raise from the seeds may not look exactly like the parent. To some people, that matters. To me, it doesn't. I plant the seeds anyway, and if the plant grows into something I don't like, I pull it up and put it in my compost pile. Occasionally, I've even grown plants that I thought looked better than the parents—not often, but occasionally.

8

From the Ground Up

The soil in the area where I live is *clay*. Not just clay, but CLAY. When we first moved here, I didn't want to wait for several years to start a landscaping project while I improved my soil. I wanted an "instant garden." So that's what I got. How did I do it? By putting six-inch layers of well-rotted manure over the soil. Wasn't it hard work? You bet it was! But it was worth it. And the best part was that the manure was free. Of course, I had to go to the site, shovel it into the truck, drive home, and unload it, but as I mentioned previously, I rationalized that the cost of gas and time were equal to the cost of a membership in that exercise class I had planned to take. What better way to lose weight than to do it improving the soil? Of course, if your soil is perfect, you can skip this section and go on to the next. But I feel sure that there's not much soil that can't stand some improvement.

The instructor who told my class that a perfect soil would result in six years if six inches of well-rotted manure were added to the soil as a mulch every year didn't take my impatience into account. I didn't want to wait six years, so I got my calculator and figured out that if twelve inches were put on every year, half in the fall and half in the early spring, the process would take only three years. So I planted by gardens, then started to improve my soil, and it worked. My calculator was right.

If you've done any reading on the use of manure to enrich the soil, you might be concerned that this would cause a nitrogen deficiency. It won't, unless you plan to mix the manure in with the soil. I was much too lazy to rototill the manure into the soil and, besides, I had already put in a lot of plants and it would be impractical even to try to till around them.

The same rule goes for sawdust. If it's used as a mulch, it doesn't cause a nitrogen deficiency. If you're going to work it into the soil, just make sure it's well-rotted. If not, to prevent a nitrogen deficiency, for each inch of sawdust you put on, you should spread one pound of ammonium sulphate for each one hundred square feet of area. In the second year, use half as much ammonium sulphate, and in the third and fourth years, one-quarter as much. If you use manure, you have to use twenty times as much ammonium sulphate. And to top it off, each year the amount should be made in several applications. All of this is too complicated for my calculator to handle, so I just get whatever I can find for free and put it on top of the soil. Over the years, I've used quite an assortment of mulches.

Where do I find all this free mulch? Usually, it's available just for the asking. You can use any number of things as mulch. For instance, what accumulates faster than old newspapers? "Yuk," you say, "who wants to look at a yard covered with newspapers? And anyway, they'll just blow around and make a mess. Besides, what will the neighbors think?" The neighbors need never know. Just put the newspaper down in layers and cover them with something else—say barkdust, if that's the "in thing" in your neighborhood. Everyone around here uses it and does anyone know that I've only got a shallow layer of it on top of newspapers? Do you know how much a load of barkdust costs these days? Think of all the money you'll save. If you attempt this method, however, you can save yourself a lot of work by wetting the paper first or undertaking the project on a calm day when rain is forecast.

Some people use black plastic under barkdust, but in my opinion old newspapers are preferable. Didn't you ever wonder how plants breathe with plastic all over the soil? Also, how do they get enough water? Sure, there's a small area around each plant that's left open, but what happens when the plant grows and the roots spread out past the opening? The soil around the hole is covered with plastic and probably gets mighty dry, so the water that makes its way into the hole has to moisten a large area. Or if the plant is at the bottom of a slope, all the water will drain that way. Then how does it evaporate? It doesn't. This creates a sour soil in which most plants are loathe to grow. A newspaper mulch will let the plants breathe and not sour the soil. Of course, you should not put on a six-inch layer of paper as you would with manure. An inch will do nicely. And don't use the color sections of the paper, only the black and white. I know, I know, some authors swear that black plastic is the best thing since the advent of the power mower. I don't. But that's just my opinion.

LET YOUR FINGERS DO THE WALKING

You don't like the idea of newspapers? Then how about leaf mold? Do you remember I talked about this in chapter 5 on wildflowers? Well, the rest of your plants, not to mention the soil, would benefit from it too. You can get it from several sources. Of course, if you know someone who owns property in the woods, the source is obvious. Just remember that leaves such as oak create very acidic humus. Don't put it around plants that don't like acid soil like aster (*Aster* various), baby's-breath (*Gypsophila paniculata*), carnation (*Dianthus caryophyllus*), clematis (*Clematis* various), dahlia (*Dahlia* various), daphne (*Daphne* various), delphinium (*Delphinium* various), hawthorn (*Crataegus* various), hollyhock (*Alcea rosea*), monkshood (*Aconitum* various), peony (*Paeonia* various), or poppy (*Papaver* various). If you have no country friends, bring out your phone book and call any nearby universities. Ask the maintenance department where the leaves that are collected every year are dumped. Try the city and state too. A lot of agencies are beginning to compost their leaves, but there are often too many to handle and they are more than happy to get rid of some. If you have a choice, take the ones from the most rotted area. If they're not at least partially rotted, you might want to compost them for a while or they're likely to blow away. As an alternative, you could throw a few shovels full of soil over the leaves to help hold them in place.

While you have your phone book out, look for other places you can call for mulching materials. If you want manure, call boarding, rental, racing, state, or county fair stables. How about the animal science department at the local university? Then there are feedlots and dairies. Just imagine how much manure they accumulate. One dairy near here gives coupons for free manure to a grocery store. If you buy a certain amount of groceries, you are entitled to a coupon for a specific amount of manure. However, if you get manure from a poultry farm, be aware that this type of manure is much stronger than horse or cow manure and needs to be weathered well before it is used. You could, of course, apply it in late fall so it has a chance to weather on the ground. When using any manure, keep it off the leaves of plants and keep it a distance away from the trunks too. Better safe than sorry, since it could burn your plants.

If you have a choice of getting manure that has been mixed with straw or some that has sawdust in it, by all means take the sawdust, especially if you're going to do the hauling and spreading. The sawdust/manure combination is much easier to shovel and seems to break down faster. I also prefer the looks of it. With straw, there always seem to be clumps that make the yard look unkept.

Do you have a farm bureau cooperative in your area? Call and ask if they have anything that would be suitable for use as mulch. You don't have to ask for something specific. Let them tell you what they have. A friend of mine in the Midwest gets ground corn cobs from such a cooperative. And since she is the first one who has asked, she got the several-year-old stuff that had been sitting at the back of the lot and was well-rotted. She said it was just like good soil—rich and black.

Then there's mushroom compost. Lately it seems to have become a rather controversial subject. Mushroom compost is just composted horse manure that has been used to grow mushrooms. Since mushrooms sometimes have to be sprayed for disease and insects, many people don't want to use the compost as mulch. They also say that since mushrooms are fertilized, there are a lot of fertilizer salts left in the compost that could damage plants. But then there are the people on the other side of the fence who say they have been using mushroom compost for years with nary a problem. I'll let you decide. My opinion is that if it is used in combination with other mulches, and in moderation, it might not be as bad as some say. I don't use it because so far I haven't found a free source. But if one came along, who knows? I might give it a try. However, I wouldn't use it on my vegetable garden.

Try calling tree pruning services. Tree pruners are especially good sources for mulch after a bad storm. They have chipping machines that can make wood chips out of a fallen tree in no time. The city, state, and even the electric company has chippers. I know a man who made a deal with a landscape maintenance company's chipping crew. If they were within a five-mile radius of his house and had a load of chips, they would drop them off in his driveway and he would give them a six-pack of beer. That sounds like a reasonable enough deal to me.

Sawmills are a good source of sawdust and sometimes even barkdust. In our area, the mills burn the barkdust as fuel during most of the year. But when the rainy season comes, the barkdust gets wet and it's not feasible to use it as fuel. Then the mills are almost eager to give it away. If you get turned down at one mill, call another. Usually sawdust is yours for the hauling. Sawdust that comes from home power saws probably won't work as well. It's so fine that it tends to form a crust that water can't penetrate. If you have a free, plentiful supply of it, mix it with something else—leaf mold, manure, what-have-you, and you'll get much better results.

In our area, there are many filbert orchards. What happens to all the shells? I called to find out, and now some of them are in my yard. In other areas, you might be able to find pea pods or even winery waste. Keep your eyes open and you'll be amazed at what you'll find. And ask, ask, ask. Let everyone know that you're looking.

You could try running an advertisement as one person here did. He asked for grass clippings and even gave an address where they could be delivered. I think that's taking it a bit far, though. Also, I would specify that I wanted only those that were unsprayed. If you've never worked with grass clippings, be careful of the black plastic bags into which everyone seems to put them. If the temperature is the least bit warm, the clippings will start to decompose in no time and create a stinky, slimy mess. Get them out of the bags as soon as possible and don't put them into piles or the same thing will happen. If at all possible, spread them out to dry or put them immediately onto the beds as a thin layer of mulch. Of course, you'll probably get weed seeds along with the clippings, but that's the price you have to pay. You'll probably find weed seed in most of the mulch you get, with the exception of nut shells, wood chips, sawdust, or the like. However, in my mind all this mulching effort is worth it. There's nothing nicer than to push a shovel into your flower bed with just a slight bit of pressure. It beats having to dig a hole with a pickax.

TO COMPOST OR NOT TO COMPOST

I read quite a bit about composting before I actually tried it. The more I read, the more complicated it sounded. You have to add things in layers, mix it often, take its temperature, keep it from drying out, keep its feet from getting wet, and on and on. It seemed to me to be more trouble than taking care of a sick child. Then one of the women who was doing volunteer gardening with me told me how she does it. She uses a garbage can, cuts out the bottom, turns it upside down, puts in kitchen scraps (no meat, of course), lawn clippings, weeds, garden prunings, a bit of soil, and whatever else she has on hand. She does this in no particular order and at no particular time. Occasionally she'll add a shovelful of manure if she has it, and once in a while she will leave the lid off when it's raining. After reading all the sophisticated directions in books, it sounded too simple to me, but I tried it anyway. It worked. A short while after I had filled the garbage can (which I picked up free at that "Dump Day" I told you about), I lifted it up and I had wonderful compost. The only thing I changed on the second batch I made was that I tried to keep the pieces smaller and omitted larger woody branches. The smaller the pieces are, the more quickly they decompose. On my next batch, I'm going to throw in a handful of earthworms and see if they help get the job done any faster. Needless to say, after my first success, I was on the lookout for old garbage cans. I now have a team of six working full-time and am contemplating more. I even lucked out and got five of those at once. A friend of mine had a small trailer court and needed new cans when the bottoms rusted out of the old ones. Had I not told her earlier that I was looking for them, she would have taken them to the dump. This, by the way, is a fantastic place to look for garbage cans. Unfortunately, the dump in our area is closed to people who want to take things out. You can only dispose of articles, not pick them up. Dumps in other areas are not so stringent with their regulations. Check out the one near you. My dad lives in another state and visits his dump regularly. He calls it his "warehouse." He's discovered what he's needed to make everything from a shredder and rotating compost barrel to a cold frame. Every time he goes to his "warehouse," he comes back with treasures.

If you can't scrounge for garbage cans in the dump, you could run an advertisement in the paper for them. Save someone a trip to the dump and say you'll pick them up within a so-many mile radius of your home. As far as plastic cans are concerned, I really don't know how well they work. I've never tried them, but it seems they would work just as well.

What do you put into your compost cans? Just about any soft vegetative material. If you own fish tanks, when you change the water, use the old water as moisture for your compost can.

When you weed, you can throw weeds in too. I leave a little soil on the roots of the weeds and rationalize that this will add enough to the can so that I don't have to put in an additional shovelful.

Why bother with composting? Why not just mulch with the material as it is? Good question. As I already mentioned, you can do this with many things. But kitchen scraps, for instance, or weeds, would not exactly enhance your landscaping and might attract mice or rats. One advantage of compost is that it is already broken down into soil and its nutrients are more readily available to the plants—and it will improve the soil more quickly. Either way works—it's up to you. I particularly like to use compost in my vegetable garden because I know the plants will not be in the ground a long enough time to get the value of a layer of mulch. I still mulch my vegetables to conserve moisture and hold down the weeds, though, not to provide nutrients to the plants.

KEEP SEEKING AND YE SHALL FIND

What else do you use when you garden? Tools, right? Where can you get them very reasonably? Besides at the "warehouse," go back to garage sales, estate sales, and auctions. Of those, estate sales are probably your best bet. You can stop at a lot of garage sales before you find one that has lawn and garden equipment, but almost any estate sale will have some unless it's an apartment or condominium—or if the relatives took it all. Of course, estate auctions would have them too, but at an estate sale you don't have to spend time waiting for the items to come up, you can purchase them immediately. Often, however, you might get a better price at an auction. Just be prepared to spend some time there. Sometimes the garage is the last area the auctioneer goes into during the sale. As with the nursery auction, people don't bid as avidly at the end of the sale, so you have a good chance to buy what you want at a reasonable price. The disadvantage is that by this time the auctioneer is probably tired too and may lump things together into what he calls "lots." You might have to buy several things you don't want in order to get something you do want. If you're a horse trader by nature, this will prove no problem—you can put an advertisement in the paper to sell the unwanted items, or trade them. I've done this and ended up making more money selling what I didn't want than what I paid for the whole lot in the first place. On other occasions I've gotten stuck with a collection of unsaleable items. In any case, horse trading is not for everyone.

Some gardeners are like some cooks. They have a different tool to do each job. I don't. First, I can't afford them, and second, I have no room to store them. Here are the basic tools with which I garden. Maybe this will give you new gardeners an idea of what to watch for at flea markets, garage sales, auctions, and such. And don't turn your nose up at used tools. Often the older ones are made better or of a higher quality material (see Figure 8-1a and b).

I have only one type of garden fork. It's called a spading fork and is especially good in heavy or rocky soil. I use it to turn and break up the soil. To me, it's also essential when I dig bulbs and divide perennials because it seems to do less damage than a shovel.

Two kinds of shovel are indispensible. One is a spade with a blunt end for rough digging, opening soil, and leveling. The other is a standard garden shovel to dig holes and move soil.

I also have two types of rakes. I use the level head rake to level and smooth surfaces and collect loose material such as rocks or dirt clumps. Obviously, a leaf rake is used to rake leaves and clippings. To me, it doesn't matter whether the leaf rake is metal or bamboo—both do the same type of job, one as well as the other.

Since I do very little weeding using a hoe (believe it or not, I enjoy hand weeding), I don't even own one. Besides weeding, though, a hoe can also be used to cultivate and make seed furrows (I use a stick). Since I don't use a hoe, I can't recommend one style over another. All I know is that there are many different types available.

In the line of hand tools, all I have is a trowel. I'm rather hard on my trowels, and my husband was tired of unbending them for me, so he finally found a good old-fashioned model at a thrift shop. He paid a whole dollar for it and it has lasted me for years. I use it for any kind of small scale digging I do, whether it's digging dandelions out of the vegetable garden or planting annuals in my flower border.

As far as pruning tools are concerned, here is where it really pays to get good-quality equipment. Nothing is harder on a plant than dull or poor-quality equipment. You know how hard it is to cut a piece of meat with a dull knife? It's the same with pruning tools. You want to cut a branch off, not butcher it. I have four pieces of pruning equipment, all of which I find indispensable. I use pruning shears to remove shoots and small stems, lopping

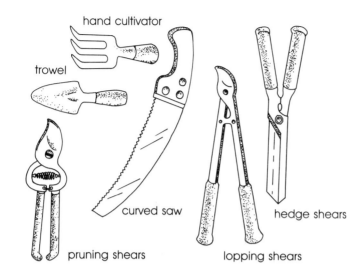

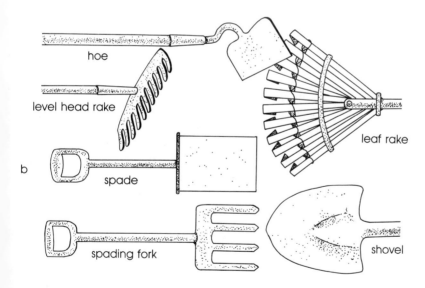

Figure 8-1 (a and b). Garden tools you will need.

shears with long handles for larger stems, and a curved pruning saw for large branches. Whatever you do, don't try to cut large diameter branches with pruning shears. Not only do you run the chance of ruining your shears, but you'll probably injure the plant as well.

The fourth pruning tool I use is a hedge shear. Mine is manually operated. Since I don't have much hedge to trim, I can't rationalize spending the money on an electric model. They also don't seem to work well on hedges with lots of thick, woody stems because they bind up and shred the stems. Some plants that gardeners often shear are: privet (*Ligustrum* various), boxwood (*Buxus* various), laurel (*Laurus nobilis*), heath (*Erica* various), and heather (*Calluna* various).

In the line of watering apparatus, I pretty much use the nozzles, hoses, and sprinklers that I find at sales. However, in the vegetable garden, since I have raised beds, it's easiest for me to put a soaker hose down the center of each bed in early spring. Then, when it comes time to water, I turn the soaker hose on quite low so that it waters only the bed, not the aisleways in between. That way, I not only conserve water, but I also don't have as many weed problems in the aisles because they get no water all summer.

I don't believe in gadgets, but one I can't live without is a little plastic shut-off valve. I put it on the end of my hose and can shut off the water wherever I am without having to walk back to the spigot. I consider that a luxury, even though it only cost me ninety-eight cents on sale.

I also use soaker hoses in parts of the yard where it's difficult to water with a conventional sprinkler. It seems that there's always one corner that's impossible to get and that's exactly where the soaker hoses come in handy. I suppose if I had a small yard I would use them throughout, but since I don't, I use the oscillating type of sprinkler. It's the one that goes back and forth. I know that some experts say that the rotating type (around and around) is much better, but every time I try to use it I get frustrated (and wet). It just seems I can't get it to sprinkle in the right pattern. My yard isn't round—it's rectangular. With a circular pattern, there's always four corners that don't get watered. If I overlap the pattern, there are some places that get overwatered. Maybe I should take a class on the basics of watering with a rotating sprinkler.

As far as wheelbarrows are concerned, I like the old-fashioned deep ones best. They seem to hold more than the newer plastic models. Of course they are heavier, since they're made of metal, so if weight is a factor, definitely look for the shallower plastic types.

When it comes to buying tools, I don't always buy something just because it's cheap. I feel that the old adage "You get what you pay for" applies here. If it only costs a dollar but the handle is cracked, I weigh the cost of a new handle against the probability of getting my husband to replace it within the next year. Then I multiply that number by the amount of trouble it will be to go to a store to purchase a new handle. Using this formula, I often pass up the "bargain."

Another thing to check tools for is rust. If the problem is only on the surface and the rust has not pitted and scarred the implement, I often will buy it—if it's a super deal, of course. I use solvent and steel wool on the rust, and if there are a few nicks, I take them out with a steel file. I don't use the formula I just mentioned on this type of purchase because I already have steel wool, solvent, and a file on hand and also because I don't have to depend upon my husband to do it.

Speaking of tools, a long time ago a magazine I subscribed to had a helpful hint that a reader sent in. He said that he kept a pail of sand saturated with motor oil handy and each time he finished using a tool, he plunged it in and out of the sand a couple times. This, he said, kept this tools clean and they stayed sharp longer. I tried it and it worked. I also rub the metal parts of my tools with oil before I store them for the winter. The way I figure, if I buy good tools, I might as well take care of them and make them last. If the tool is not so good, it needs all the help it can get to keep it going.

Keep your eyes open for other things at estate sales—pots often go very reasonably. I went to one at the end of the day, inquired about a boxful of clay pots and was told that since no one else had expressed an interest in them, I might as well have them. The sellers didn't want to go through the bother of taking them to the dump.

When it comes to purchasing chemicals at sales, watch out. A nursery or greenhouse sale is okay, but be careful at estate or garage sales. You don't know how many years they've been sitting around, whether they've been tightly closed, or even if they've accidentally been frozen. Some chemicals are good for only a limited time after they are opened, and some are useless after they've been frozen. Fertilizers aren't quite as fussy and are usually all right unless they've been wet.

Remember that mulch breaks down to form soil, so it has to be constantly renewed. Tools will get broken or lost, chemicals and fertilizers used up. You should always keep an eye out for replacements. When something is free or cheap, don't pass it up just because you don't need it at the moment. Practice stockpiling against a rainy day. If nothing else, you can use it as trading stock. All this may sound complicated, but after you've gone through the procedure it will come naturally and you'll become a seasoned (and successful) gardener.

9

In the Beginning

As you began to read this book, you logically assumed there would be an end to it. There is none. Landscaping is an ongoing process. Once you get everything where you want it, it's time to mow the lawn, fertilize, and prune. Or you find that you've changed your mind and really don't like where you put this or that. Perhaps, after all, you aren't quite so fond of a plant you thought you couldn't live without and want to replace it with something else. Or maybe you've seen a new variety that you just have to have.

You might find you want to do more reading on how to divide your plants. After a few years, many varieties will need this. And the time may come when someone will walk by as you are working in your yard and say, "My, that's a lovely plant. Would you mind telling me what it is so I can go to a nursery and get one?" That's your clue that someone else has read this book, and it's time for you to know how to divide the plant, how to slip it, or if it should be propagated by seed. It's also a clue that this person is another scrounger. Ask what he or she has to trade for the plant that is desired. Fair's fair, right? Of course, if your fellow plant enthusiast is just starting out and has nothing to trade, don't be hesitant to give him or her a start of what you have to offer. You can never tell when a person will come upon a find and remember your generosity.

GIVER'S GAIN

Speaking of giving, once you get hooked on plants, you'll find that they are very handy, inexpensive, and much appreciated gifts. Even the novice can dig up and pot a clump of parsley or chives during the warm months to use as a gift. You can also bring some plants inside in pots to set on a sunny window for use as winter presents. More advanced gardeners will find dozens of useful and unusual herbs that most people are delighted to get. I'm especially fond of the scented geraniums that come in all types of fragrances—from apple to old spice to rose. They are particularly nice to give to someone in the hospital because the fragrance will help to cover up the scent only hospitals have. And yes, scented geraniums can really be used as flavoring in cooking. In winter, a sprig of lemon geranium is a lot less costly than a real lemon. I wouldn't try to make an apple pie from apple-scented geranium though—that's taking it a bit far. But just imagine what you could do with lime, nutmeg, cinnamon, coconut, ginger, orange, strawberry, or almond-scented geraniums. I have a catalog that lists more than fifty scented varieties. Let your imagination run wild.

Why not start to learn to cook with herbs? Even if you're like I am and would rather be gardening than cooking, when I compare the cost of a box of herbs from the store to the cost of a plant (which I hope after reading this book you will get for next to nothing), it makes me want to learn to cook with the fresh herbs. There is a difference between using fresh and store-bought herbs, you know. The flavor of the fresh is by far superior. You can even save the woody stems from your garden herbs and throw them into the fireplace or barbecue for a pleasant fragrance. Or mix dried spices and herbs that are past their culinary prime and place them in a jar with a tight-fitting lid. Keep this next to the fireplace and throw in a handful when you want to fill your house with summertime fragrances.

You can even freeze whole mint leaves or small violet (*Viola* various) or borage (*Borago officinalis*) flowers in ice cubes to garnish cold drinks for a special treat. Now wouldn't that impress your mother-in-law?

Then, of course, you might find that you have so many plants in bloom that you can cut armloads of lovely flowers to bring into the house. In this case, of course, you'll have to learn about cut flowers—which will keep longest, which drop nectar, pollen, or petals; which need to have the stems singed or mashed to keep longer. You'll need to find out how to arrange them so they look like the ones in a florist's window. Again, get your answers at the local library. You'll find books on arranging cut flowers, preserving them, using dry flowers, making potpourri, creating dried flower wreaths, and even which flowers are edible. One of my favorite edibles is the brightly colored nasturtium (*Tropaeolum majis*). It lends a peppery flavor to tossed green salads and brightens them up too. Or use chives (*Allium schoenoprasum*) flowers instead. They add a more subtle lavender color and a slightly oniony flavor.

One of my favorite herbs and one that isn't too well known is lovage (*Levisticum officinale*). This is a perennial that is grown for its celery-flavored seeds, leaves, and stems. You can't stuff it as you would real celery, but for everything else it works just fine. I use it in egg salad, soups, meatloaf, spaghetti—anything that calls for cooked celery or celery seed. I also dry it to use in winter. Then when I see the price of a bunch of celery in November, I just smile and put aside the amount I would have spent on it. Later, when my seed catalogs come, I can splurge on something I can't find and I don't have to feel guilty about it.

THE NOSE KNOWS

Fragrance is becoming a more important factor in the home today. In medieval times, fragrant herbs and flowers were used to cover up the odors that were so prevalent before sanitation was improved. Today a wonderful scent has the potential for making your home more attractive and lends a relaxing atmosphere. Try tucking muslin sachets of fragrant flowers behind your funiture's cushions. Or plant fragrant bulbs like freesia or hyacinth in pots and force them into bloom in the winter. One pot can perfume an entire room.

If you're going to force bulbs, don't try to use those that have been thrown out by someone else. They probably are not in top condition and have come from crowded beds. They will not give you the best bloom and may not even bloom at all if forced. Break down and buy (wholesale, if you can) the largest size you can. Usually they are called forcing bulbs. Before you buy, however, check Table 9-1 to see which varieties are especially recommended for forcing. Then purchase them at a reputable place and ask if the particular ones you picked out are suitable for forcing, if they're not listed in the table. The best time to prepare the bulbs is in early fall.

Now that you have the bulbs, the next step is to plant them. A good soil consists of equal parts of sand, peat, and soil. The pot that you use must have drainage holes and be at least four inches deep. As far as the pot size, the bigger the bulbs, the bigger the pots need to be. Grouping the bulbs several to a pot seems to produce a better display. For example, put six daffodil bulbs in a

TABLE 9-1

Good Bulbs for Forcing

Daffodils:
  Bicolor—Bath's Flame, Foresight, Irene Copeland, John Evelyn, La
    Riante, Patricia, Rustom Pasha, Texas
  Pink—Maiden's Blush
  White—Beersheba, Cabtatrice, Daphne, Eskimo, Mt. Hood
  Yellow—Carlton, Dutch Master, Fortune, Golden Harvest, Hunter's
    Moon, King Alfred, Magnificence, President Lebrun, Unsur-
    passable
Hyacinths:
  Blue—Blue Danube, Blue Jacket, Christmas Bells, Delft's Blue, Duke of
    Westminster, King of the Blues, Ostara, Perle Brilliant, Vanguard,
    Winston S. Churchill
  Pink—Anne Marie, Lady Derby, Marconi, Pink Pearl, Princess Victoria,
    Queen of the Pinks, Rosalie
  Red—Cyclop, Delight, Fireball, Garibaldi, Jan Bos
  Violet—Amethyst
  White—Blom's Gem, Carnegie, Colosseum, L'Innocence
  Yellow—City of Harlem, Gypsy Queen, Yellow Hammer
Tulips:
  Orange—Apricot Beauty, Orange Wonder
  Pink—Christmas Marvel, Peerless Pink, Pink Perfection, Rose
    Copeland, Weber
  Purple—Van der Neer, William Copeland
  Red—Bing Crosby, John Vermeer, Olaf, Paul Richter, Scarlet Admiral,
    Scarlet Cardinal
  White—Hibernia, Joan of Arc, Pelican, White Sail
  Yellow—Bellona, Golden Age, Golden Harvest, Mon Tresor, Orna-
    ment, Safrano, Thunderbolt
Others:
  Crocus, Freesia, Grape Hyacinth, *Iris reticulata*, Squill

ten-inch pot, or six crocus bulbs in a five-inch pot. Larger bulbs such as tulip, hyacinth, or daffodil should have about one-half to one inch of space between them. Smaller ones such as crocus and freesia may almost be touching.

Put soil in the pots to a depth that will allow you to put one-half inch of soil on top of the bulbs. All bulbs need to be covered except for daffodil whose necks can be allowed to protrude slightly. Once the bulbs are planted, tamp down the soil and water. Special bulb pans are available by the way. They are more shallow than standard flowerpots and also usually more expensive.

Now it's time for the cold treatment. The bulbs you potted need a cool, frost-free area to sit in for a time until their roots develop. About 40 to 45° F. is optimum. Do not water them again unless they become dry. Some gardeners say that putting them in a dark place is not important as long as they are kept cool. Others say both cool and dark is imperative. I use cool and dark just to be on the safe side.

Leave the pots in this spot until the leaves start to show through the soil, or until you can see roots through the drainage holes of the pot. This is a signal that the bulbs are ready for the next step. With tulips or daffodils, wait until the leaves are about two inches high. If you have them in a dark place, the leaves will be yellowish, but don't worry about it. They will soon green up. If you're in doubt about whether or not it's time for the next step, wait a couple more days. It's better to leave them in the cold too long than to try to force them too early. Remember, they need plenty of time to develop a good root system.

The next step is to increase the temperature. You can accomplish this by taking them into your house. If you want to prolong your bloom period, try bringing in one pot each week. That way, when one pot is fading, another is just beginning to bloom. When you first bring them into the house, put them in the darkest corner of your room for a few days so they can acclimate to the light. Of course, if you've had them in the light to begin with, this step is unnecessary. In this case, put them in a sunny place but try to keep the temperature below 70° F. At night, a temperature below 60° F. is best. The cooler the temperatures, the longer the flowers will last. Keep them moist, and in about a month you should have a wonderful array of fresh flowers. Force hyacinths or freesias and they will be fragrant, too.

Once the flowers have faded, keep the plant in a sunny spot and continue to water it when it becomes dry. When it warms up enough outside so that there is no danger of frost, put the pot out in an unobtrusive place, stop watering, and let the leaves die back. Don't try to force these same bulbs again next year—they're all tuckered out. You can plant them in the garden, however, and they'll bloom there.

MAY THE FORCE BE WITH YOU

Do you know how expensive fresh flowers can be in the winter? Rather than purchase them for the special occasion you need your house decorated for, plan to force some branches out of your yard (or your neighbor's). Tell them that you will do some of their pruning for them by selectively cutting the branches. Many types of plants will provide free color for your house if treated correctly. Try forsythia (*Forsythia* various), pussy willow (*Salix* various), flowering quince (*Chaenomeles* various), apple (*Malus* various), cornelian cherry (*Cornus mas*), February daphne (*Daphne mezereum*), or flowering cherries, plums, or almonds (*Prunus* various).

If you need the branches to be blooming at a specific time, remember that they will take about two weeks from the time of cutting to bloom. The later in the season it is, the less time it will take.

Cut two- to three-foot branches from January to March. The warmer your climate, the earlier you can take the cuttings. If you're cutting from someone else's bush, be sure that you cut just above a node. That way, there won't be any dead stumps left for them to be disgruntled over and maybe next year they'll let you do it again. When you take the cuttings, you should be able to see the little flowerbuds swelling up.

After the branches are cut, smash the cut ends with a hammer. I know this sounds cruel, but it actually will enable the plant to take up water better. Place the branches in water and put them in a cool (less than 70° F. is best), bright, but not sunny area. Change the water frequently and in about two weeks you'll have spring flowers in the middle of winter.

Some perennial plants can be forced in much the same way as bulbs. Try plantain lily (*Hosta* various), bleeding heart (*Dicentra* various), astilbe (*Astilbe* various), or sweet violet (*Viola odorata*).

Dig flowerpot-size clumps in early fall and trim off at least half of their height. Put these clumps in pots in standard house plant potting soil, water, and put the pots in a cold frame. If you don't have one, try making one (or getting your husband to) out of a discarded storm window (see Figure 9-1). If you don't care to go the cold frame route, you may put them into an unheated garage or attic—anywhere that the temperature won't go below freezing. At the end of January, bring the pots inside to a sunny area where the temperature will stay below 70° F. Keep the soil moist, and after the leaves actively begin to grow, fertilize the plant twice a month with regular house plant food. After the clumps have bloomed, replant them in the garden. Just don't try to force these

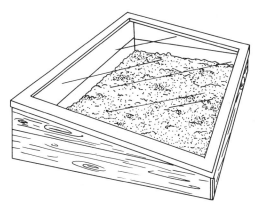

Figure 9-1. A cold frame.

clumps again. Since many perennials benefit from being divided, perhaps a neighbor would allow you to do some dividing work in exchange for a couple clumps of her plants.

Want to feel really luxurious? Make your own bubble bath. All it takes is a mild soap, like Ivory Snow flakes and rose petals. Or you can use any fragrant flower—try lily-of-the-valley (*Convallaria majalis*), heliotrope (*Heliotropum arborescens*), lilac (*Syringa vulgaris*), freesia (*Freesia* various), or even the fragrant narcissus (*Narcissus* various). Run a little very hot water in the tub, then add about one-half cup of the soap. Put a handful of the fragrant petals into a square of cheesecloth or the toe of an old nylon, secure it to the faucet (I use a rubber band), turn the water on full force, and voilà, you have bubbly fragrance—very relaxing. The cost? A fraction of the price of commercial bubblebaths. And there are no harmful additives.

You can even make this concoction as a gift. Use empty fruit jars or similar containers with tight-fitting lids. Make layers with Ivory Snow granules (granules work better in this case) and petals until the container is filled. Tightly seal and store in a dry, dark place until needed. To make the gift prettier, transfer some of the preparation into more attractice bottles or jars, add bows, and you have a very personalized, unusual present.

Ready to try something a little more exotic? How about candied mint leaves, rose petals, or violets? Just coat individual flowers with beaten egg white, put them into a bowl, and sift sugar over them until the flowers are well-covered. Place them on a tray lined with wax paper and let them dry in an airy place for a day. Then turn them over and leave them until the other side is dry too. This is a fun project for a little girl and is a nice gift for her to give to "someone special."

I hope I've turned you on to some of the endless possibilities of what can be done with plants. Acquiring plants is only the beginning. There is always something new to learn. Once you get hooked on plants, you'll find more and more fascinating things about them and more and more uses for them.

Maybe someday we'll meet in an alley in a pile of discarded tulip bulbs. Now, though, I think it's time for me to go out to the garage and pot up some daffodils. I'm going to force them to use as presents. Let's see now, I'll use the free pots I got at the fair, the free soil from the landscape conference, the four dozen named variety bulbs I got for two dollars at an auction, and the bone meal I bought at wholesale price from a bulb company catalog. Four bulbs per pot gives me twelve pots of "brand-new" daffodils for three dollars and a little time. That's twenty-five cents a pot. Where can you get a more beautiful gift for less money? Can't beat a deal like that!

This is not the end—but hopefully for you it is the beginning of a whole new adventure.

A
Pennypincher's
Calendar

JANUARY

- Make want lists of seeds, plants, and tools. Don't forget to make a dislike list too.
- Go through your garage, attic, cupboards, etc., and accumulate unused items for a spring rummage sale. Promise yourself that all your profits will go toward your landscape projects.
- Cut the limbs of your Christmas tree to use as winter protection for perennials and bulbs.
- Ask your friends and neighbors for Christmas plants they have received that are past their prime. Most people throw them out. You can recycle them. Typical Christmas plants you can acquire in this way are poinsettia (*Euphorbia pulcherrima*), Christmas cactus (*Schlumbergera bridgesii*), begonia (*Begonia* various), cyclamen (*Cyclamen persicum*), Jerusalem cherry (*Solanum pseudocapsicum*), and ornamental pepper (*Capsicum annuum*).
- Save your wood ashes (or get your neighbor's).
- Keep feeding the birds.
- Continue to bring in bulbs you have potted for forcing.
- Bring in branches of flowering trees and shrubs to force.

FEBRUARY

- Take in your pruning shears and lawnmower for sharpening. You won't need them much now, and hopefully you'll get better quality work done because the individual doing the job won't be rushed with an overload.
- Start a seed trading group with gardener friends and neighbors. Often, you don't want a whole package of seeds, so you can get more variety by trading half your package for someone else's unneeded varieties.

- Collect old cookie sheets, egg cartons, etc., to use to start seeds indoors.

- Watch for sales on fruit tree dormant sprays and pruning equipment.

- Purchase seeds of early starting cool-weather vegetables (on sale, of course). Look for peas, onions, spinach, endive, radish, and cress.

- In warm winter areas, plant bare-root shade and fruit trees. Don't fret when you have to pay for sticks. I promise you they'll leaf out and you save money by buying them bare root. If, perchance, they don't leaf out, don't be afraid to take them back to the nursery and ask for a refund or exchange.

- Take cuttings of deciduous shrubs, grapes, and berries for progagation.

- Bring in cuttings of flowering trees and shrubs to force.

MARCH

- Make plant tags on a cold, blustery night. This is a great project for kids while they're watching television. Using cottage cheese containers, cut out the top ridge and the base section. Then vertically cut whatever size labels you want from the remainder. Later, you can use a grease or lead pencil to write plant names on them.

- Start a compost can with the winter mulch you rake off your plants.

- Bring in branches of flowering trees and shrubs to force.

- Watch for sales on Easter azaleas (*Azalea* various) and lilies (*Lilium* various). Ask friends for their discards.

- Look for annual and herb seed, perennial and shrub sales.

- In cold winter areas, plant bare-root shade and fruit trees.

- Make a plan for your vegetable garden. Consider talking a friend into growing more of one plant and none of another. Then grow what your friend didn't and exchange. For instance, if she has no room for cucumbers and you don't have luck growing carrots, you could try this deal.

- Keep an eye out for sales of bare-root roses.

- Take geraniums (*Pelargonium* various), dahlias (*Dahlia* various), and gladiolas (*Gladiolus* various) from storage.
- Start tuberous begonias (*Begonia* various) indoors.
- Apply wood ashes to your vegetable garden at an annual rate of about two pounds per one hundred square feet.

APRIL

- Gladiola (*Gladiolus* various) corms should be on sale now.
- If your soil needs improvement, check for advertisements for free manure in the classified section of the newspaper.
- On sunny days, watch for garderners dividing perennials such as plantain lily (*Hosta* various), delphinium (*Delphinium* various), coral bells (*Heuchera sanguinea*), chrysanthemum (*Chrysanthemum morifolium*), summer phlox (*Phlox paniculata*), michaelmas daisy (*Aster novi-belgii*), shasta daisy (*Chrysanthemum superbum*), daylily (*Hemerocallis* various), primrose (*Primula* various), and peony (*Paeonia* various). If you don't know how to approach the people dividing them, re-read the method in Chapter 2.
- Take a walk in the woods and tag plants for later transplanting.
- Watch for lettuces that do well in hot weather to go on sale.
- Summer flowering bulbs such as canna (*Canna* various), begonia (*Begonia* various), tuberose (*Polianthes tuberosa*), Peruvian daffodil (*Hymenocallis narcissiflora*), and achimines (*Achimenes* various) should be on sale now.
- Trade vegetable starts with friends to get more varieties.
- Power equipment often goes on sale now.

MAY

- Garage sales abound at this time of year. Scout for pots, tools, and plants.
- Hold your own garage sale and don't forget to earmark the profits for future landscaping projects.

- Bring out the poinsettias you scrounged in January.
- Sales of perennial and vegetable starts are in full swing now.
- The same applies to tool sales.
- Watch for gardeners thinning and transplanting their bulbs.
- Seasonal nurseries often have clearance sales at this time of year.
- Add your grass clippings to the compost can.

JUNE

- While on vacation, collect interesting stones for a rock garden or wildflower seeds to grow.
- Annual plants go on sale now. So do bare root roses.
- Save your grass clippings (unsprayed, of course) to use as a mulch to keep the soil temperatures down during the hot months to come.
- Be sure to eat your thinnings of lettuce, onion, and chard.
- Watch for sales on chemicals.

JULY

- Spring flowering bulbs should be on sale now.
- Ask gardeners for softwood cuttings of shrubs such as heath (*Erica* various), heather (*Calluna* various), evergreen azaleas (*Rhododendron* various), and rose (*Rosa* various).
- Gardeners are usually dividing their bleeding heart (*Dicentra* various), bugloss (*Anchusa azurea*), and oriental poppy (*Papaver orientale*) now. Need I say more?
- Continue to collect mulch to use to protect ornamentals from hot weather damage.

AUGUST

- Take cuttings of plants such as coleus (*Coleus hybridus*), fuschia (*Fuschia* various), and geranium (*Pelargonium* various) to be carried over the winter.

- There should be sales on cool season vegetables such as lettuce, fall broccoli, Chinese white winter radish, and Chinese cabbage now.
- Plan to trade vegetables with gardener friends who may have an overabundance of a different variety of vegetable than you have.
- Sometimes there are clearance sales on garden tools at this time of the year.
- Watch for gardeners dividing their hardy garden lilies (*Lilium* various).

SEPTEMBER

- Start freesia (*Freesia* various) corms for forcing.
- Watch for gardeners dividing their iris (*Iris* various), peony (*Paeonia* various), chrysanthemum (*Chrysanthemum* various), dahlia (*Dahlia* various), aster (*Aster* various), primrose (*Primula* various), and gladiolus (*Gladiolus* various) plants or storing their geraniums (*Pelargonium* various) and begonias (*Begonia* various).
- There should be sales on roses and perennials now.
- Make Christmas gifts such as pickled cherry tomatoes, lavender bath salts, herb jellies, salts, and vinegars.
- Build a cold frame.
- Collect manure.
- Cut plants for winter arrangements and drying.
- Go back to the woods and dig the plants you marked in the spring.
- Take a walk in the country or check vacant city lots for Queen Anne's lace (*Daucus 'carota'*), cattail (*Typhus latifolia*), teasel (*Dipsacus sylvestris*), and ornamental grass to cut for arrangements.
- Spring blooming bulbs should be on sale now.
- Collect leaves for use as mulch later.

OCTOBER

- Prepare bulbs for forcing.
- Dig perennials for forcing.
- Pot herbs such as parsley (*Petroselinum crispum*), chives (*Allium schoenoprasum*), scented geranium (*Pelargonium* various), and thyme (*Thymus* various) to carry through the winter in the house.
- Keep an eye out for sales on fruit trees, shade trees, and shrubs.
- Watch for clearance sales on tools and chemicals.
- Gardeners should be dividing their lily-of-the-valley (*Convallaria majalis*) and rhubarb (*Rheum rhabarbarum*) now.
- Bring in and store tuberous begonias for their resting cycle.
- Save your Halloween pumpkin's seeds for the birds. Harvest sunflower heads for them too.
- Slug bait should be on sale now.
- Consider planting shrubs and trees that offer food and shelter to birds, such as sumac (*Rhus* various), barberry (*Berberis* various), and holly (*Ilex* various).

NOVEMBER

- Mulch with the leaves you've collected after the ground is frozen or in mild winter areas when the daytime temperatures are usually below 50° F. Do not use leaves from fruit trees. These should be destroyed to prevent spread of leaf diseases.
- Check stored flower bulbs for rot or fungus problems.
- Send for seed catalogs or trade with gardening friends. Even if you don't plan to buy from the catalogs, they're full of information and ideas.
- Decide which new garden areas you will need next year and spade or rototill them.

DECEMBER

- Start to bring in the bulbs you have potted for forcing.
- Collect ashes and store them in a dry place.
- Prune your evergreen trees and shrubs and collect cones to make Christmas decorations. Take out crossing branches. Cut them back to a joint or the trunk so that the wound will be concealed by other growth. Mash the ends of the prunings and set them in water until you are ready to work with them.
- Cut berried shrubs and holly for decorative purposes. Holly (*Ilex* various) should be dipped in a hormone solution called alphanapthalene acetic acid to help it maintain its leaves and berries. This hormone is available from nurseries and garden centers.
- Find a free source of chipped tree limbs to use as mulch.
- Feed the birds. Save your squash and pumpkin seeds for them.
- Consider garden-related Christmas gifts for the gardeners on your list.
- Have a happy holiday season.

Index

Y